With love from Ishkel to Khrissie

W9-CMN-474

JESUS — POWER WITHOUT MEASURE

To the MacPhail Family

D1117098

Jesus — Power Without Measure

The Work of the Spirit in the Life of our Lord

J. DOUGLAS MACMILLAN

One of my favourite Preachers

EVANGELICAL PRESS OF WALES

© Evangelical Press of Wales, 1990
First published 1990
ISBN 1 85049 074 0

All rights reserved. No part of this publication may be reproduced, stored in a retrieval system, or transmitted, in any form or by any means, electronic, mechanical, photo-copying, recording or otherwise, without the prior permission of the Evangelical Press of Wales.

All Scripture quotations are from the New
International Version except where otherwise indicated.

Published by the Evangelical Press of Wales
Bryntirion, Bridgend, Mid Glamorgan, CF31 4DX
Printed by Billings and Sons Limited, Worcester.

To

the congregation of St Vincent Street Free Church of Scotland, Glasgow, whose loyalty and love moulded my ministry from 1974 until 1982, and with whom the subject was first shared in sermonic form, this work is warmly dedicated: and especially to the memory of Ian Bain, deacon, appreciative hearer and recorder of sermons and, in his own quiet way, friend, counsellor, and weekly encourager of his minister, early and suddenly removed from the church on earth in the summer of 1989. Without his work for the tape ministry, reflecting his own desire to share the gospel, it is unlikely that this book would ever have been written.

Contents

1
The Mission of Jesus

*'And now the Sovereign LORD has sent
me with his Spirit'* (Isaiah 48:16).

The importance of the subject

The idea that the Holy Spirit is intimately involved with the
ministry and work of Christ is probably familiar to most
Christian believers. It could hardly be otherwise. Matthew,
Mark, and Luke all speak of the Holy Spirit in connection
with the birth, baptism, and temptation of our Lord. Even so,
it is all too easy to miss the wider implications of this involve-
ment, and its significance for the work of Christ as the
Redeemer and Saviour. That significance lies in the unques-
tionable truth that there was a ministry of the Holy Spirit
with, in, and through the Lord Jesus Christ all through his
life and in every aspect of his saving work.

Long before the coming of the Lord Jesus in the incarnation, Scripture speaks of a mission of the Spirit which has the
closest affinity with the saving work of Christ in the world. So
closely identified are they that in the above quotation the twofold commission from the Lord God to the Son and the Spirit
inaugurates one single, joint engagement. The sending of the
Spirit which is in view is to be linked with, and locked into,
the mission of the Son when it occurs. There are definitely
two persons spoken of here, but only one sending. The inference we are invited to draw, therefore, is that the two are
being sent out with the same aim, and to accomplish the one,
great, divine purpose.

9

This inference is entirely legitimate and, in fact, is confirmed by Scripture in a wide variety of ways. Its teaching on the Spirit's coming and having a part in the ministry of Christ in this world is firm and explicit and, once we begin to look for it, extensive. Moreover, the Spirit works in such a fashion as not to detract in the slightest from the redemptive enterprise, or the redemptive accomplishment, of the Son. In complete harmony with a principle running through all the Spirit's work, this ministry veils itself and shines the spotlight of revealed truth upon the Saviour. The principle on which he conducts his mission is voiced by the Lord Jesus: 'He will not speak on his own . . . He will bring glory to me' (John 16:13,14). That is a chief characteristic of all the Spirit's work in the world and in the church. That may be one reason why the subject is a strangely neglected one, seldom dealt with in contemporary preaching or Christian literature. But that is a good reason, in itself, to take it up and examine it.

Light on the person of Christ

Two thoughts are absolutely basic and fundamental to the biblical teaching on Christ, and they are found in both the Old and New Testament witness. So crucial are they to that witness that they must both be accommodated in any serious interpretation or evaluation of Christ and his work. Failure to do justice to either one of them distorts that witness and so, inevitably, falsifies our understanding of Jesus. We fail to get the true picture.

The first of those two thoughts is simply that Jesus, although genuinely human, was also a *divine* person. That teaching has, of course, from the earliest time, been the subject of much probing and testing and preaching and writing in the Christian church. It is so deeply rooted in Scripture and so clearly a part of orthodox Christian belief from the very beginning, that it has withstood every attack of unbelief. Every believer who has come to know Jesus as Saviour rests in him, and on him, in the full assurance that he is God. Christian experience underwrites and confirms the teaching of Scripture. The trust that is engendered by saving faith compels the soul to fall down in worship before this Jesus and say with Thomas, 'My Lord and my God!' (John 20:28).

The second thought bears more directly upon the theme of this book. It is one which has received far less attention than the other. Strangely enough, this is probably because men have often felt that it posed a threat to the teaching on his divinity and Godhood. It is the fact that Jesus was the anointed Servant of the Lord.

The doctrine of the 'Servant role' of Christ, and the thought of his being the specially anointed Servant of the Lord, automatically draw attention to Jesus as man. The focus is on his need of being equipped, empowered and strengthened in this Servant role. It is precisely this thought of servanthood, and the conditions intrinsic to it, such as subordination or dependence or need, which have made people draw back almost instinctively, with the feeling that such ideas are untenable in association with one who is really and truly God. Yet the Bible witness demands and requires such association and, for a very profound reason, teaches that those conditions were, and had to be, part of the life-experience of Jesus. The reason is simply this: Jesus was just as truly *human* as he was *divine* — he was man as well as God: he was the God-man. But as man he was also Servant. An essential aspect of the incarnation is not understood if this is not grasped. The apostle stresses this element of Christ's humiliation very strongly, saying that he 'made himself nothing, taking the very nature [form; belonging to the essential nature] of a servant' (Philippians 2:7).

This, of course, points up the complexity of Christ's 'twofoldedness', which is given theological formulation as 'two natures [one human, one divine], but one person'. And this is what distinguishes him from all others who have ever lived on earth. His own claims in this direction and the Bible's emphasis on them, both in historical narrative and predictive prophecy, mark him off from all other men and from all other religious leaders. This is his singularity, his uniqueness. He was God's Son and he was God, but for the purposes of our salvation he became one with us. Such oneness with us

11

was an essential element of his mediatorial office and work. Furthermore, it was true, and real, and absolute, except for sin. But, and this is crucial in Christology, his oneness with us did not cancel out his oneness with God. Incarnation did not involve any negation of his deity. 'He became what he was not,' said Augustine long ago, 'but did not cease to be what he was.'

It will already be apparent that our subject bears very directly upon the doctrine of Christ's true manhood. Far from involving the orthodox doctrine of Christ in any embarrassment, it actually reinforces that doctrine and helps clarify the broader-based teaching of Scripture from which it is drawn. To deny, or diminish, the full humanity of the Saviour is, after all, just as unbiblical, just as heretical, and just as wrong as it is to deny his full deity. The teaching of the Bible on the true humanity of Jesus is very plain and explicit, but it can sometimes be pushed into the background. This is especially true at times when the deity of Christ is challenged, as it has been (even within the church) over the last hundred years or so. The doctrine of the work of the Spirit in Christ will help us keep a proper biblical balance and perspective in our thinking about Christ. In a number of ways, it is essential to the holding of a full-orbed and biblical Christology.

Light on the work of the Spirit

The subject also involves, of course, the person and work of the Holy Spirit. Looking at what his anointing and filling of Jesus involved will help us appreciate, from a broader perspective, some of the biblical principles which apply to *all* his works in this world and, in particular, in the renewal, sanctification, and anointing of the Christian believer. To probe his ministry in the life of the Son (as Scripture reveals it to us), and to come to some understanding of its purpose, its effects, its extent, and its principles of operation throw light on the work of the Spirit in other areas.

The Bible makes it clear that the Holy Spirit has a place and a part in all the works of God, and this strand of biblical teaching on his activity in the divine administration has been articulated in a very simple, straightforward, theological formula; this is how it is expressed: 'All things are from the Father, through the Son, by the Spirit.' It is important to understand the force of that formula and the truth it expresses. It points us on to the thought that the Holy Spirit is the agent and the executor of the divine will. He is personally involved at the point where the divine purpose of the triune God is brought to actualization. His special task is to bring to completion and perfection the works of Godhead in every sphere.

This is beautifully illustrated in the sphere of man's redemption. The apostles take for granted (so much so that they everywhere assume our assent to their outlook) the general corruption of man's nature and so refer, again and again, to the Spirit as the instigator and source of all the saving, sanctifying, and comforting influences which belong to true Christian experience.

The beginning of the Christian life, over against the former unconverted, sinful life, is uniformly ascribed by the New Testament to the work of the Holy Spirit. Says Paul, 'No-one can say, "Jesus is Lord," except by the Holy Spirit' (1 Corinthians 12:3), and again, 'He saved us through the washing of rebirth and renewal by the Holy Spirit' (Titus 3:5). The message of the Bible is unmistakable. It is this. The work of the Spirit *in* us is just as necessary as the work of Christ *for* us. They are not contrary to each other in any way, but complementary aspects, the one subjective, the other objective, of our one, great salvation. Scripture often links them. For example, Paul in contrasting the pre- and post-conversion life of the Corinthians puts them together in this way, 'And that is what some of you were. But you were washed, you were sanctified, you were justified in the name of the Lord Jesus Christ and by the Spirit of our God' (1 Corinthians 6:11).

The teaching of the Bible here is straightforward and clear. It is the Spirit who quickens the soul into life and who enables it to believe upon, and rest only in, Christ for salvation. It is the Spirit who brings light to the mind, and renews the will, and with his invincible power overcomes the natural enmity of the human heart towards God and towards good. In theological terms, it is the Holy Spirit who applies the salvation which Christ has effected and completed for us. It is the Spirit who is there at the point of the application of redemption. The work of regeneration is the Spirit's work.

The Spirit in creation

That the Spirit's role in the world is on a wider scale than this is evident from Scripture. He was active, for example, in the original work of creation. Such a role comes to light in several places of Scripture. 'Now the earth was formless and empty, darkness was over the surface of the deep, and the Spirit of God was hovering over the waters' (Genesis 1:2). 'By his breath [spirit] the skies became fair' (Job 26:13). 'When you send your Spirit, they are created, and you renew the face of the earth' (Psalm 104:30). These verses show that the Spirit was deeply involved in bringing the creation to perfection.

In the creation of man the presence and power of the Spirit are again evident. The divine purpose, expressed in the words, 'Let us make man in our image, in our likeness' (Genesis 1:26), was realized by the activity and power of the same Spirit. 'The Spirit of God has made me; the breath of the Almighty gives me life' (Job 33:4). This is an obvious reference to the better known words from Genesis 2:7, 'And the LORD God formed man from the dust of the ground and breathed into his nostrils the breath of life, and man became a living being.' The Hebrew word for spirit, *ruach*, denotes a breath, a wind, or an intelligent, thinking being. But it is clearly God's Spirit who is at work here, and when we read 'the breath of *life*' (or more specifically, '*lives*', for it is plural) we must understand that man is being put into possession of life in the Holy Spirit as well as physical and intellectual life. In other words there appears to have been an imparting of 'spiritual' life in this action (with a filling of the Spirit implied, as well). Doubtless, we are not able to understand, or analyse, precisely what qualities were imparted to man, but they clearly will include all that definitively sets humans off from the other creatures. Any interpretation of the biblical evidence at this point must reckon with the special qualities implicit in the special pronouncement and the special action by which the creation of man is so distinctively indexed. Whatever else may be involved, the words certainly convey the idea of a highly distinguishing and specializing creative activity on the part of the Holy Spirit when man was made. The distinction can best be understood, and finds its most cogent exposition, along the lines of man's moral, intellectual, and spiritual life. The verse quoted from Job undergirds the view that here, at the very point of man's animation into all that makes him man, the Holy Spirit was present and active as the executor of this great divine purpose.

The Spirit and the Trinity

Inevitably, our subject has a bearing on the tri-unity of God. The very groundwork of the Spirit's work in the Lord Jesus compels consideration of the distinction of persons involved in the work of redemption.

Those activities of the Spirit in creation and in the application of redemption illustrate that the Spirit is always involved at the point where the works of God are actualized. Our interest has centred on the fact that the Bible represents him as the agent of Deity. This must not lead us into thinking that the Spirit acts alone, or in isolation from the other persons of the Godhead. Such ideas cannot be maintained in the face of the biblical teaching on God as Trinity. Trinitarian doctrine has to be set aside if any of the ongoing works of God are not represented as being common to the three persons.

This biblical emphasis on the executive role of the Holy Spirit must not be misconstrued. The activity of the other persons is not being excluded. In the ultimate analysis, all the varied works of the Almighty have to be reckoned as the single act of one God. Trinitarian theology does not believe in, or teach, three Gods, but one; and that one God existing eternally as Father, Son, and Holy Spirit. But the point is that just as there is distinction of persons but no division of nature in the Godhead, so there is distribution of labour but no division of purpose attributed by Scripture to the divine activity in creation and redemption.

15

Once we appreciate this executive role of the Holy Spirit in those two spheres it becomes natural to look for his presence in other spheres as well. That will be the aim as we examine different aspects and facets of the work and ministry of the Spirit in the life of our Lord Jesus Christ.

The Spirit as the anointer of Christ

Looking at the work of the Spirit in the creation of man points to a fundamental truth about the incarnation of the man Christ Jesus. The very idea of man implies a constant agency and work of the Spirit in Jesus. The first Adam had a plenitude of the Spirit until that indwelling was forfeited by sin. But man was made to be filled by the Spirit and to know his presence and power. More especially is this so when the man in view is 'holy, blameless, pure, set apart from sinners' (Hebrews 7:26). There was nothing in this man, as there is in every other man, to offend or grieve or quench the Holy Spirit of God. Neither was there anything in him, or done by him, to forfeit the power and anointing of the Spirit as is true of all other men. All others have to say, as David the psalmist said, 'Surely I have been a sinner from birth, sinful from the time my mother conceived me' (Psalm 51:5). In Jesus it was the very opposite, in and from his conception.

There are radical differences between this indwelling of the Spirit in Christ and that in the believer. Those differences are important in helping us understand the utter fulness and plenitude of the Spirit's anointing and power in him.

First of all, even in the most holy and gracious and obedient Christian believer, the Holy Spirit always meets with the resistance of evil. There is still in every one of us what we may call the entail of sin. But the heart of the Lord Jesus was always without sin, and his life without any taint of unrighteousness at all. In his sinless human nature the Holy Spirit met with no resistance of any kind, no resentment, no refusal.

Secondly, no Christian is ever filled to 'plenitude' fulness with the Spirit. His operations, influences, support, and leading in our fallen human nature are always partial and so

16

incomplete. But with Jesus this, again, was not the case. He could be — and was — filled with the perfect plenitude of the Holy Spirit — above measure, or 'without limit' (John 3:34). In him the indwelling of the Holy Spirit was central and complete, leaving no void or vacancy.

Thirdly, in us the Holy Spirit meets with an ego, a self-centredness which opposes God, which is proud and self-reliant, even in the Christian. In the person of Jesus the Spirit came and filled a man who was perfectly holy and whose human nature was ready, always, to give perfect co-operation to all the promptings, leadings, and guidings of the Spirit.

The messianic title of Jesus

This anointing ministry of the Holy Spirit in the Lord and Saviour should not be found surprising. The very title under which the Old Testament prophets predicted his coming and under which his believing people looked for him pointed directly towards it. He was to be the Messiah — which is the Hebrew for the Anointed One. His New Testament title — Christ — is just the Greek form of that Old Testament name, in fact a direct transliteration of the original *Christos*. This is the form in which it was written and read in the Greek translation of the Old Testament and so the idea of anointing was woven very deeply into messianic expectation many long years before his actual coming.

It is all too easy to overlook how strongly Scripture stresses this thought of the Spirit's anointing of, and his resting upon, the Servant of the Lord. But it is, in fact, fundamental to the work of Messiah; so much a part of it that the anointing becomes the characteristic from which the messianic office finds its title. Isaiah, especially, sheds light upon the ministry of the Spirit in Messiah. 'The Spirit of the LORD will rest on him — the Spirit of wisdom and of understanding, the Spirit of counsel and of power, the Spirit of knowledge and of the fear of the LORD' (Isaiah 11:2). 'Here is my servant, whom I uphold, my chosen one in whom I delight; I will put my Spirit on him' (Isaiah 42:1). 'The Spirit of the Sovereign LORD is on me, because the LORD has anointed me to preach good news to the poor' (Isaiah 61:1).

When taken together, those passages are very informative about the purpose of Christ's anointing and, although that purpose is spelled out for us by way of predictive prophecy, no clearer description could have been given of the actual accomplished ministry. Their application to the life of Jesus is put beyond doubt by New Testament references. The second, for example, is cited by Matthew in relation to Jesus' ministry of healing. It was all the historical realization of what Isaiah had said: 'Here is my servant whom I have chosen, the one I love, in whom I delight; I will put my Spirit on him' (Matthew 12:18 ff). The last passage is applied by Christ to himself in assertion of his messianic authority and works (Luke 4:17 ff). The gifts and graces enumerated in such predictive Old Testament passages are all gifts of which the Holy Spirit is the sole author, and which are found in their perfection and plenitude fulness only in Messiah, only in the Spirit-filled, Spirit-anointed man Christ Jesus.

The question has sometimes been agitated as to whether this anointing was only of Christ's human nature or whether it was of his person. The graces spoken of are all of the kind which would be found in a person and, apart from the person of the eternal Son of God the human nature which he had assumed into union with himself had no identity. It did not act, or even exist on its own. It was body and soul, but it never was the body and soul of any other but the Son of God. It was his human nature, so all the actions, and ministries, and deeds, were personal. Perhaps we come close to the actuality if we say that, so far as the *call* to messianic office is concerned the person of Christ was anointed; for the *execution* of that office supplies of gifts and graces, abilities and powers are required. To that end his human nature was anointed.

Interesting and important issues arise out of our subject. Covering the ground will involve that fascinating range of prophecies about the Anointed One and their final exposition in the person and work of our Lord Jesus Christ. The theme is, in fact, sharply focused and succinctly summarized in some memorable words recorded by the great historian of the New Testament, Luke. They are actually the words of the disciple Peter, and they tell us, with beautiful simplicity, how the prophecies became real in the world and its history; he speaks about 'how God anointed Jesus of Nazareth with the Holy Spirit and power, and how he went around doing good and healing all who were under the power of the devil, because God was with him' (Acts 10:38).

2
The Incarnation of Jesus

'The Holy Spirit will come upon you, and the power of the Most High will overshadow you. So the holy one to be born will be called the Son of God' (Luke 1:35).

That is the way the greatest of all miracles, the incarnation of the eternal Son of God was announced and explained to Mary, the one person in the whole world most intimately involved in it. From her, and through her, God's only begotten Son was to become man. It was a question from Mary herself which prompted this explanation of what was to take place; and her question — 'How will this be . . . since I am a virgin?' — has, for other reasons than hers, and in very varied forms, found its echo in many hearts ever since that time.

Incarnation — the humiliation of Christ

His entrance into the human condition, his becoming a true man, his living in a fallen, sinful world, all meant self-abasement for the glorious Son of God and we must never underestimate the cost of that action. The details and circumstances of his birth emphasize, in their own quiet way, the humiliation involved. The family into which he came was poor; the man who was to act as his earthly father was a manual worker rather than from among the ruling class; his birth was in a stable or cowshed; all this is eloquent of the very radical change of state that incarnation involved for the Lord Jesus Christ.

20

It must not be thought that his humiliation started only when men began to desert him and plan his removal by violent death. He humbled himself just by taking human nature. His conception and birth involved a state of humble, creaturely dependence. Although that is a continuous state, it is one in which we can trace progressive descent to the place where further investigation is forbidden. It has plunged to depths where man has never been. But even in the assumption of our nature he was taking, so to speak, a downward step. God could not become man and not be involved in humiliation.

Abraham Kuyper has expressed these truths very powerfully and cogently. He writes, 'His self-emptying was not a single loss or bereavement, but a growing poorer and poorer, until at last nothing was left Him but a piece of ground where He could weep and a cross whereon He could die. He renounced all that heart and flesh hold dear, until, without friend or brother, without one tone of love, amid the mocking laughter of His slanderers, He gave up the ghost' (Abraham Kuyper, *The Work of the Holy Spirit*, Grand Rapids, Eerdmans, 1956, p.107).

It is important to remember that in becoming man Christ did not do anything that was grossly degrading to him as the Son of God. Nor was he doing anything not predicted of him in messianic prophecy. In the course of the church's history men have sometimes taught that the idea of the eternal God becoming man is grotesque and is not a fit doctrine for the belief of a morally sophisticated or ethically refined religion. Apart from the obvious answer that it is a biblical doctrine, and that without the teaching of the Bible man is hardly in a position to know what is seemly or unseemly for God, there is another important consideration that such reasoning ignores.

This is the biblical teaching on what man is and how man was when he came from the hand of the Creator. When that teaching is given its full and proper place, then there is nothing grotesque or unseemly or blasphemous about the doctrine of the incarnation. This is so because the humanity that the Son of God took into union with himself was pattern-

21

ed after the image and likeness of God. In taking human nature into personal union with himself he did not link himself into a nature that was alien to Deity, such as the angelic nature, but one moulded upon his own essential and personal glory because man was made in God's image. There is nothing grotesque or unseemly about that.

In the biblical doctrine of incarnation, as well as that of the exaltation, there are basic factors which must not be forgotten or our whole understanding will be distorted. One of those factors concerns the scriptural teaching on the beginnings of human life. That indicates a special place of dignity and honour for man in the creaturely order of things. God's gracious purposes of redemption and salvation, centring as they do upon the human race, and focusing upon the work of the Son, set the value and worth of men at an enormously high premium. The biblical interpretation of man — both in his origins and destiny — always views him as in a special relation to God and his love in Jesus Christ. Thus, as far as the Son is concerned, incarnation must mean humiliation, but cannot mean degradation.

Two more factors require emphasis. The first will be a recurring theme throughout this book; that is, how real and actual Christ's humanity was, and is. The ministry of the Holy Spirit in Jesus, when we grasp its implications, should imprint that very strongly upon our minds. But his being filled with the Spirit 'without limit' also indicates how close an affinity there is between a personal God and the personal attributes inherent in human nature. It demonstrates, not merely that there is nothing incongruous about God becoming man, but also that man is a creature capable of receiving the anointing and indwelling of the Holy Spirit and being endowed with gifts and graces which give uplift to human character and adorn human personality. The incarnation, and the Spirit's ministry in the man Jesus, both sit well with the biblical view of man as a spiritual being.

The second emphasis is by way of safeguarding our understanding of Christ's deity, lest it be overshadowed by the stress on his manhood throughout these chapters. Although

22

the Son of God was found in human nature, living and working as man, we must not imagine that there was a vacancy in the throne of heaven. His coming in human nature was a movement, an extension, down from the throne but he was still one of the persons of triune Godhead. And as the Son of God he still had the divine attribute of omnipresence.

Not only does he speak of himself as the Son of God who is in heaven while he was the Son of Man on earth, but incarnation did not, and could not, involve him in laying aside any of the essential attributes of his deity. Had it done so, it would no longer be true incarnation and he would not have been the God-man. We may put it like this: there was no vacancy in the Trinity because the Son became man; and the Son was still everywhere present as God, although as man he was also walking the roads of Galilee in humiliation.

Incarnation — the sending of the Son

The angel's message to Mary deals with the deepest and holiest mystery, and the greatest miracle, recorded in the New Testament. While Jesus of Nazareth is, without any shadow of doubt, a real historical figure, the constitution of his person and the Christian understanding of him are matters, purely and simply, of scriptural revelation. That revelation declares him to be the Son of God come in our nature; the God-man, unique, and different from every other man who ever lived, yet truly one with them.

This doctrine cannot be considered apart from another — that God exists in the unity and diversity of Trinity. The incarnation, though inexplicable, is not incredible. As is the case with the Trinity, the scriptural data by which the doctrine of Christ — *two* natures, but *one* person — is established are not found in any single text or place in the Bible, but it is a necessary inference from three sets of broadly-based scriptural assertions. First, Jesus Christ was properly and literally a man; second, Christ is also properly and literally divine; and third, this God-man is one and the same person. Every text speaking of Christ, for example, either asserts or implies, the unity of his person, and his possession of personal attributes.

23

In certain passages some proposition asserts both natures in one person; for example: 'I have spoken to you of earthly things and you do not believe; how then will you believe if I speak of heavenly things? No-one has ever gone into heaven except the one who came from heaven — the Son of Man' (John 3:12,13). There are many such texts in the New Testament.

Our text emphasizes that the one to be born of Mary as the result of the overshadowing power of the Holy Spirit would be holy, and that he would be called the Son of God. 'The power of the Most High' is synonymous with and explanatory of 'the Holy Spirit'. God is to exercise his divine power through the Holy Spirit who will be the executor and agent in its application and exertion. The presence of the Spirit here reflects, as in the first creation, a creative and perfecting role.

Another matter must be emphasized very strongly. It is this: the text does *not* teach — nor does the Spirit say — that as a result of his conception in the womb by the overshadowing power of the Spirit, Jesus will *become* the Son of God. Rather as a result of this supernatural conception, and the birth in which it will issue, he will, in his humanity, reveal himself and declare himself as a divine Being. He will be acknowledged as such and will be called Son of God. But before his miraculous birth he was *already* the Son of God. This means that there is a Sonship that belongs to our Lord quite apart from his becoming man; a Sonship which goes back beyond his human birth or its inception; a Sonship which is pre-temporal, non-creaturely and, consequently, eternal. This important truth has a corollary: to deny that the Lord Jesus was eternally the Son of God, is to deny that the Father was eternally the Father.

If God is the eternal Father, then, of course, there has to be a Son — one of whom he is the eternal Father. And a major stress of scriptural teaching on the sending of a Saviour is laid upon the fact that it was the Son who was sent. Again and again we read that God sent his Son. To question that the Lord Jesus was the Son is to detract from what Scripture declares as a very special love; this love is magnified, measured, commended to us just because it was the Son who was sent — who was not 'spared'. The greatness of the gift is the very thing which advertises the greatness of the Father's love. There, at the heart of this great mystery of the incarnation, is another; the mystery that God could love sinners like us, and love us to this extent. That is the overwhelming mystery — and it is the mystery which interprets and justifies and even explains the other mystery. It does not explain *how* it took place, but it does explain *why*, and the explanation is so enormously comforting that, even where we do not understand, our hearts are won and we can trust, and not be afraid.

Incarnation — the sent one, truly Son of Man

The presence of the Spirit at the point of incarnation, as the anointing Spirit, is significant for another reason. It heralds the genuine character of the human nature that the eternal Son assumed into union with himself. It is humanity, not deity, which needs this anointing and all that it implies. This creative work of the executor of the divine purposes is implied in Psalm 40, and from that place is applied by the writer to the Hebrews to the conception of Christ's human nature: 'Therefore, when Christ came into the world, he said, "Sacrifice and offering you did not desire, but a body you prepared for me"' (Hebrews 10:5).

Apart from this body, incarnation would not have taken place. But the reality of Jesus' manhood is crucial, not merely to the reality of the incarnation, but because it introduces true human perfection into the world. This is what the situation demanded; it is what Christ's mission required. The Bible stresses this 'natural' unity with mankind — this sharing of our nature, and so of our experience. 'For surely it is not angels he helps, but Abraham's descendants. For this reason he had to be made like his brothers in every way, in order that he might become a merciful and faithful high priest . . . and that he might make atonement for the sins of the people' (Hebrews 2:16,17). There is an absolute, essential conjunction between Christ and his people.

Jesus became true man. Incarnation is not the appearance

25

of a man; nor is it deified man. He had a 'true body, and a reasonable [rational] soul' (*Westminster Shorter Catechism*). It might be assumed that this required some sort of transmutation of what he was and had been eternally; that his becoming man would require some modification, some reduction, of his full, majestic, glorious deity. Indeed some have thought that his becoming man meant a merging of the divine and the human. But all such suggestions fall short of the biblical witness. Comprehensive analysis of that establishes his true and proper manhood, and one way in which it asserts the factuality of his manhood is by the ministry of the Spirit in the theanthropic person, the God-man.

One of the things that men have always admired about the teaching of Jesus is its high moral and ethical standard. What they have not always appreciated is the marvellous way his whole life undergirded that teaching and made it vigorous. Despite their admiration, they have found that they were powerless to attain that standard and that those who have most nearly approximated the ideal that Jesus taught are the very ones who have been most deeply persuaded of their failure. Yet the uniform testimony of the New Testament witness is that he, himself, embodied the standards and ideals he taught. In him men saw to perfection that love to God and neighbour around which his ethical requirements revolved. As no other religious leader ever did, Jesus the Saviour lived what he taught, and taught what he lived. He lived as God intended man should live.

Incarnation — the birth of a sinless man

In delivering his message the angel does not merely announce that the incarnation of Christ will take place through the direct influence of the Holy Spirit, but also expressly declares that the man to be born will be free from all taint of sin. He will be the Holy One. While he was to be a real human, like us and one with us in everything, the Lord Jesus was also to be enormously and magnificently unlike us in one particular. He was to be like us in everything except our sin. If there is a conjunction between Christ and his people there is also a dis-

26

junction between them. This is how the New Testament expresses it: 'We do not have a high priest who is unable to sympathize with our weaknesses, but we have one who has been tempted in every way, just as we are — yet was without sin' (Hebrews 4:15). Everything else in human experience was to be fully shared by him with that one exception, and that one exception underlies all his work for us. It is one of those features which make him a great Saviour.

That exception is one reason why the incarnation took place in the way it did. The Son of God assumed human nature by being born of a virgin — no human father being involved. He did not come into the world as men usually do. In an age sceptical of all things supernatural, some feel encumbered and embarrassed by the doctrine of the virgin birth. Two things must be said by way of response; first, it is a biblical doctrine; second, in the face of other gospel doctrines, this one is not out of character. Given the truth of the incarnation — that Jesus was the God-man, then there is really nothing very surprising, or at all incongruous, about his being born in this unique and special way. The miracle of the coming of God's Son into the world in our nature outstrips the miracle of its method by far. It is hard to understand why men take in their stride the fact of the incarnation yet stumble at the manner of the incarnation. This is to swallow the camel while straining at the gnat. We should be aware, also, that the scriptural teaching on the coming of the Messiah had hinted, and more than hinted, had long ago openly declared, that his birth would be unusual and that not man, but woman, would be the one from whom the 'seed' or 'offspring' would stem on the human side.

The very first intimation to man of a coming Saviour was by divine promise. The wording of that promise singled out the importance of *woman* in his coming. In doing so, it pointed to an unusual birth and even to the exclusion of the normal role of man. It was of the seed of the woman that it was said, 'He will crush your head, and you will strike his heel' (Genesis 3:15).

When we move on to the prophecy of Isaiah and its declaration of the coming Messiah we find some other interesting thoughts conveyed. For example, he speaks of both a birth and the gift of a Son; 'For to us a child is born, to us a son is given, and the government will be on his shoulders. And he will be called, Wonderful Counsellor, Mighty God . . .' (Isaiah 9:6). When Isaiah, earlier, speaks of how the given Son will come, woman is again mentioned. 'Therefore the LORD himself will give you a sign: The virgin will be with child and will give birth to a son, and will call him Immanuel' (Isaiah 7:14). Interestingly enough, although it is often said that Paul does not teach the virgin birth of Christ, it is certainly implicit in one of his great statements on the incarnation: 'But when the time had fully come, God sent his Son, born of a woman, born under law, to redeem those under law, that we might receive the full rights of sons' (Galatians 4:4,5).

The sinless state of Jesus is traced back to the sanctifying power of the Holy Spirit at that point of his conception. That is the meaning of the text above this chapter. The overshadowing of the chosen girl by the Holy Spirit and the exercise of creative energy which that overshadowing implies, was to issue in the birth of a holy, sinless child.

A parallel passage on the birth of Jesus should also be noted in connection with his sinlessness. Its message is complementary to that of the text: 'An angel of the Lord appeared to him in a dream and said, "Joseph son of David, do not be afraid to take Mary home as your wife, because what is conceived in her is from the Holy Spirit"' (Matthew 1:20). The general impression of both passages, quite apart from their immediate, contextual application, is to convey to their readers that the conception and birth of Jesus were extraordinary; that they did not occur as the result of the will or action of man, but as the consequence of a special work of the Holy Spirit.

This is not to be taken to mean, as some have interpreted it, that the Holy Spirit was the father of Christ. Such representations have to be rejected because they destroy the biblical teaching on the Trinity, and run completely counter to the way Jesus always spoke of the Father. This is seen, for example, in such sayings and assurances as: 'I will ask the Father, and he will give you another Counsellor to be with you for ever — the Spirit of truth' (John 14:16,17). What the Bible emphasizes is that the Holy Spirit was the efficient cause of the child's being conceived by Mary, and in this way it excludes the activity of man. This is entirely in harmony with the fact that the person born of Mary although truly man was unchangeably the Son of God. The exclusion of a human father broke the ordinary line of descent from Adam. So Jesus was in himself free from the racial guilt of sin.

It should be emphasized here that the sinlessness of Jesus did not depend upon the mother having an 'immaculate' nature, and that there is not even the shadow of such a doctrine all through Scripture. From earliest times, however, this doctrine of the Saviour's sinlessness has caused difficulties for some and has, sometimes, threatened the equally clear, equally biblical, doctrine of Christ's true humanity.

This is illustrated, for example, by the rather strange fact that some have tried to meet the difficulty they thought they saw here by virtually denying the real motherhood of Mary. She has been represented as merely a channel or pipe through which a heavenly body, immediately created by the Holy Spirit, but not formed from her substance, was born into the world. By such a birth the Lord Jesus would not have been a true man at all. He would have belonged to a different species or order of life altogether and would not have been made 'like his brothers in every way', for 'Since the children have flesh and blood, he too shared in their humanity' (Hebrews 2:14). Those difficulties have stemmed from wrong conceptions of sin, and the thought that all material substances are intrinsically evil, and so God's Son could not possibly have been a *real* man. The thought is, perhaps extreme, but it illustrates how people have shrunk from accepting real incarnation, true humanity.

What is important is that the ministry and work of the Holy Spirit at the very inception of his human life ensured that Jesus was uniquely different from all other men. In him we have the first person ever to be born into the world completely holy and free from sin. Two others had been created, but not born, sinless, and they did not remain without sin. So the Holy Spirit had a role to play, not merely in the creating of a *true* human nature for the incarnation of the Son, but a *sinless* human nature.

Incarnation — the life of a righteous man

The work of the Spirit in the incarnation of Christ is held out in Scripture, not merely as a negative but a positive element in the holy human nature which the Son voluntarily assumed and took into union with his divine person. By the Spirit that nature was endowed with all grace from the very beginning so that, although it was to be susceptible of increase as to actual exercise, no new grace ever had to be added.

The particular way in which the Spirit safeguarded the sinlessness, and ensured the holiness, of Jesus' human nature is inscrutable. Yet, there is something to be learned from the word which Luke uses of the Spirit — the word 'overshadow'. It is reminiscent of expressions or ideas used in the narrative of the original creative work of the Holy Spirit. When we turn back to that, we find that 'the earth was formless and empty, darkness was over the surface of the deep, and the Spirit of God was hovering over the waters' (Genesis 1:2).

This idea of 'movement', or 'hovering', which is ascribed to the Spirit here has been associated by many commentators with the activity of the parent bird which 'broods' or 'hovers' over its nest when hatching its offspring and cherishing its young. The concepts of presence, care, warmth, energy, and protection, have all been seen in this representation. However that may be, the figure used in the Genesis narrative certainly implies that the Spirit was bringing order out of chaos; imposing harmony, form, beauty, and meaning upon a prior stage of his creative work; bringing a cosmos out of the prevailing chaos.

The language used by Luke is surely not incidental, but rather highly significant for a true understanding of the Lord Jesus and all he came to accomplish. The Spirit who, at the first creation, brought order, harmony, beauty, and life out of the confused and chaotic, is once more active in the beginnings of the new creation, the re-creation of all things in Christ. It is altogether fitting that the Spirit who presided over the first creation — and the bringing into being of the first Adam — should be the one to preside, also, at the beginning of the new creation and the birth of the last Adam, who is to redeem it and, by his obedience and death, lay the foundations of a new order. 'I am making everything new!' (Revelation 21:5).

The presence of the Spirit of God at the birth of Christ is wonderfully reassuring. Christ was coming into this world — with all its disorder and confusion, its sin, its sorrow, and its chaos; and his coming into it as pure and sinless (essential for his mediatorial role), is under the superintendence of the Holy Spirit. He is present at the start of a work far greater than the first creation: the redemption of that creation out of the grip of evil. That is God's greatest, his most glorious work, according to biblical revelation. Here, at the outset of it all is God's Holy Spirit, brooding over it, moving in it, supervising, and ensuring that the foundations of the new order are laid in the beauty of holiness. The strategic thing about this new order is that its very foundations are laid, and are to emerge to view, in the sinless humanity of our Lord Jesus Christ.

Incarnation — God's representative man

The thought of the new order reminds us that the first Adam takes his place at the beginning of our entire situation and as the head of fallen, sinful humanity. The first three chapters of Genesis tend to be left out of today's thinking and the current evaluations of man and his environment. Yet the simple fact is that they are critical to our understanding of the entire biblical revelation, and of the gospel it unfolds for our need as sinners. In a marvellous way those chapters explain and interpret the world around us — as nothing in all the religions or philosophies of the world does.

It is over against that sombre background that the person

31

and work of Christ have to be interpreted. Christ cannot be understood outside the framework in which Scripture so cogently presents him. This is why, for example, we find Paul writing of him as the *last* Adam (not the *second*, as so many tend to say, but the *last*, because there never will be another). That expression pinpoints, precisely, the biblical doctrines of sin and salvation as they centre in those two representative men, one heading up a lost world, the other heading up a new, redeemed one.

This Adamic contrast sheds light on the biblical doctrine of Christ as the King, Head, and Priest of the new order. For that, he must not only be man, he must be perfect man. The redemption of all things is going to be achieved in the very nature which brought them down into ruin. God is going to be obeyed and magnified in human nature, just as he had been disobeyed and sinned against in human nature. The wages and debts of sin are going to be paid, very fully and completely, in the very nature which incurred them. Two Adams face each other — alike in nature but opposite in achievement.

The Holy Spirit is very much in evidence at the bringing in of the last Adam. As the Spirit of anointing he fills the human nature from the beginning. Right through the Old Testament administration of God's grace, anointing symbolized the power and the gifts of the Spirit. When David was anointed by Samuel to be king, we read: 'And from that day on the Spirit of the LORD came upon David in power' (1 Samuel 16:13). Priestly anointing is spoken of also, as typical of the limitless measure in which Jesus would be filled with the Spirit: 'It is like precious oil poured on the head, running down on the beard, running down on Aaron's beard, down upon the collar of his robes' (Psalm 133:2). At the birth of God's King and the coming of the great High Priest, it is right that the anointing Spirit be present as divine agent, implementing the set purpose of the Father: 'I have installed my King on Zion, my holy hill' (Psalm 2:6).

Incarnation — our anointed Mediator

We must understand the birth of Jesus as laying the ground-work of all his mediatorial obedience. The realization of this purpose was ensured by the unceasing operation of the Holy Spirit. All the information that the New Testament gives about the matter emphasizes and underlines this presence and this work. The marvel is simply this: over the birth of every other man and woman who ever lived is written this dreadful tale — 'conceived in sin, shapen in iniquity'; but over the man Christ Jesus this other astounding story is written: 'what is conceived in her is from the Holy Spirit' (Matthew 1:20).

When sin, and the fallenness of the world are considered, the great wonder couched at the heart of the incarnation is this; the seeming contradiction between God's Son assuming our nature and his sinlessness. The union with us is so intimate as to make him susceptible to all the temptations to which men are exposed, while on the other hand, he is completely cut off from all fellowship with sin.

On this issue there is something further to be said. There is a twofold emphasis in the biblical account of Christ's birth. The first points out that he was born of a woman — made a 'partaker' of our humanity. That is one side of the person of Christ. Incarnation constituted him one of the human race. The result of this is that we have a brother and a Mediator who has been anointed to represent his elect people before the righteous throne of God. There is a definite, specific relationship between him and us which renders his mediation available and suitable for our salvation.

The second factor strongly represented in the narrative is his oneness with God, and so, his sinlessness. That means that while we hold to the real, true humanity of the Lord Jesus, we hold with equal conviction, and upon the authority of Scripture, that this intimate union of the Son of God with our nature does not, and can not, imply the least participation in our sin and our guilt. He is man; he is perfect man; but he is also God, and truly God; therefore, as the God-man, he is the *goel*, the 'go-between', the one perfectly fitted to be our Mediator with a just and holy God.

33

Historically, the doctrine of the virgin birth has been owned and confessed in the church from the earliest times. The present denials of it from within the church are not due to any lack of scriptural evidence in support of it, nor to any doubt as to its being a part of the orthodox faith since New Testament times, but to the contemporary aversion to the supernatural. The passages of Scripture on which the doctrine is based are simply ruled out of court on the grounds of highly questionable and unsatisfactory critical views; views which would never be applied — because critically unacceptable — to any other body of literature.

Finally, the ministry of the Holy Spirit in the life of Jesus is evident from the outset. At Jesus' conception, there was a superintendence of the Spirit; there was an exercise of creative power upon the human nature; it was the Spirit who was there supplying the man Christ Jesus with all the endowments, gifts, graces, and capacities — physical, mental, moral, and spiritual — which would be required in the accomplishment of his mission. The birth of the Saviour *was* supernatural. No man could ever claim paternal relationship with Jesus. There is mystery, there is miracle, there is much which we cannot explain; and when we consider the enormity of our assertions concerning the incarnation, we need not be surprised that it should be so.

In closing, let us attend to the words in which John, the beloved disciple, describes the incarnation; as we do so, we shall appreciate our dependence solely on God's revelation for an understanding of a series of events which, without that revelation, would be totally inscrutable. 'In the beginning was the Word, and the Word was with God, and the Word was God . . . The Word became flesh and lived for a while among us. We have seen his glory, the glory of the one and only [Son], who came from the Father, full of grace and truth' (John 1:1,14).

3
The Hidden Years of Jesus

'And the child grew and became strong; he was
filled with wisdom, and the grace of God was
upon him' (Luke 2:40).

That is an attractive description of human growth at its best. As it touches, lightly and briefly, on the gradual development of the physical, mental, and spiritual elements of human nature its simplicity and economy of language convey a wonderfully complete and lively picture. The important thing is that it shows how normally the life of the incarnate Son unfolded, and how naturally the child Jesus fitted into the circumstances of his earthly environment.

Another leading feature of the description is that it singles out qualities of personality which we take so much for granted that they attract attention only in their extreme manifestations, that is, in their excellence or their absence. The first two, growth in stature and wisdom, are exactly those physical and mental developments which every father and mother wish to mark in their child. The last one, grace, only Christian parents notice, so rare is it in this sad world — which makes it all the more special when it is seen. It was those normal, hopeful signs of healthy, developing childhood, seen at their highest level and complementing one another, which marked the passing days of this boyhood.

The Holy Spirit — and the secluded experience
The short text not only characterizes developing childhood at its highest, but is one of the few, fleeting glimpses we have in-

to the life of Jesus in his first thirty years. These are spoken of by Bible scholars as the hidden years, and are of great interest and importance. It illumines the theme we are pursuing to know that Jesus, as a child, passed through the normal process of human growth. It reinforces the doctrine of his true humanity to be told that his moral and spiritual development as a child was just as real as his physical growth. In both spheres he progressed from one level of perfection to another.

This is a truth which, perhaps as much as anything else in our Lord's human experience, proves the incarnation to have been a concrete reality. While being truly God according to his divine nature, Jesus of Nazareth was just as truly man according to his human nature. Even in incarnation, God's Son is one person — as he always was, and always will be — but in incarnation he is a person who has two natures. It is necessary to insist upon the reality of the incarnate Son's humanity. So truly human is he, so much one of us, that he was completely subject to the ordinary laws of physical and intellectual development, except that in his case there was not the usual detrimental influence of personal sin.

It is perhaps because of his great gentleness, coming through to us in the Gospel narratives, that some people seem to have conceived of Jesus as rather frail in physique, and even lacking in manly attraction. It may owe something as well to the words of the prophet, 'He had no beauty or majesty to attract us to him' (Isaiah 53:2). What Isaiah has in mind is the suffering of Jesus and the agonizing nature of his death. His eye was on those aspects of Jesus' redeeming work which have been a special stumbling-block to multitudes — the scandal of the cross.

We must not entertain wrong conceptions of Jesus. If there is gentleness, it flows out of his great spiritual strength, and the calm sense of his acceptance with the Father, two things which pervade his words and works. It would be easy to contend that he was the most perfect man who ever lived, not only in the moral, but the physical realm. In form and proportion, in strength and grace of movement the world has probably never seen his equal.

The Gospels tell us that Jesus was an early riser and never easily affected by a sleepless night. As soon as it was day or, as Mark puts it, 'very early in the morning, while it was still dark', he left the house to find a solitary place where he might commune alone with the Father. This frequently followed a busy day's work (Mark 1:35; Luke 4:42). He seems often to have spent whole nights without sleep (Mark 6:48; Luke 6:12). Another indication that he was physically robust is the long journeys he made on foot. The hilly ascent from Jericho to Jerusalem, for example, called for physical exertion. It involved six hours walk, the route rising during that time to a height of over three thousand feet. Added to that were the crowds, the healing of the blind man in the morning (Mark 10:46), a hot, dusty journey through difficult terrain, and yet at the end of the day he can be at a meal with his friends at Bethany, teaching, helping, encouraging them (John 12:1,2; see 12:12).

There are other instances of his physical powers of endurance. There is the forty-days fast in the wilderness with all its strain and stress (Matthew 4:1,2). There is also his ability to go without food when his work required it (John 4:31 — even though v.6 indicates weariness after a long march). Finally, the manner in which he endured the suffering and agonies of his final night and day on earth argues for exceptional physical strength and well-being. We should not wonder at this, for from the moment of his conception in the virgin's womb, it is clear that his body, as well as his soul, was under the influence and blessing of the Holy Spirit. That is the central implication of the text.

However, it is when we examine the spiritual and moral side of his human nature that the characteristics which separate him from all other men begin to emerge. It is not possible to analyse or assess Jesus within the normal framework of human categories. This man is totally, completely, and for ever unique.

It is natural that there should be much that is deeply mysterious in the person of the Lord Jesus. It is of the very essence of incarnation that our minds cannot penetrate its mysteries, or grasp its complexities. How the same person could be at once perfect God and perfect man is a phenomenon that, itself, necessarily passes our understanding. In what measure, or in what manner, the knowledge he possessed as God was imparted to, or exercised by him as man in those early years — or even in the last years — we cannot fully understand or explain. We may go only as far as Scripture revelation permits; even then, all information is not accessible nor are all questions answered.

One prominent truth must be grasped. Our Lord shared in everything that properly belongs to man's nature, with the sole exception of sin. As man he was born an infant. As man he grew from infancy to boyhood. As man he daily and yearly increased in bodily strength and mental power. Of all the sinless conditions of man's body, from its infant feebleness, through its early growth, to its ripened manhood, he was in the fullest sense a partaker. To know this is clearly very important. Failure to appreciate it has led to many wild heresies in the past.

One emphasis of Scripture teaching that casts floods of light on the complex person of the Lord, is the one we are considering, the presence and power of the Holy Spirit in the man, Jesus. The Spirit did not, through those secluded years, abandon the work begun in preparing the constituent elements of Jesus' human nature. The opposite is true. The Spirit indwelt the child, perfecting all his human faculties, supervising each stage of their growth into maturity. His work ensured the developments the text describes and runs right through the hidden years. Jesus 'grew and became strong; he was filled with wisdom, and the grace of God was upon him'. Where grace is, the Spirit of God is also. In this instance, there was nothing to grieve or quench the Spirit, or in any way hinder his work.

The Holy Spirit — and the maturing Jesus

Scanty as the explicitly available information on the hidden years is, we can glean much by way of inference. One lesson, for example, is that the actual absence of detail proves that the Gospels were not intended to provide a biography of

Jesus, nor even the materials for it. That was not their purpose. Rather, they had only this twofold objective: that all who read them might 'believe that Jesus is the Christ, the Son of God', and that through faith they might 'have life in his name' (John 20:31).

Emerging out of those hidden years, too, are some definite evidences of the presence and ministry of the Spirit. For one thing, there is the statement in the text that the 'grace of God was upon him'. That is eloquent of the fact that the Holy Spirit was working in the child and producing those things which are pleasing to God when he sees them in men. The grace of God seen in the creature is always the fruit of the Spirit's work. Its presence signals God's favour and, especially in this instance, God's power. God's power, like his grace, is never present in any place or any person apart from the Holy Spirit. In addition, there is evidence to support an actual textual reference at this point to a presence of the Spirit and his power in the life of the child. Many early manuscripts have the reading adopted in the Authorized Version — 'the child . . . waxed strong in spirit'. The rendering 'in the Spirit' should not be ruled out.

Again, unconscious testimony to the influence of the Spirit upon him comes from the people of Nazareth, where he was brought up. Those people would know him very well, as people in small towns always do know little boys. They watched him grow, and knew his work and his family circumstances. But when he was around thirty years of age he left the town. After a few months absence he returned, and as his custom was, visited the local synagogue on the Sabbath day. What he did next was unusual and unexpected — he preached to them, and as they listened they were astounded, and soon questions were asked, 'Where did this man get these things?' 'What's this wisdom that has been given him?' (Mark 6:2).

To get the full impact of the questions we need to understand what the Jews meant by wisdom. The Greek word used, *sophia*, means lucid understanding, and scholars say was used only as expressing the highest and noblest in life. For Jews, that involved obedience to the Lord God. Their Scriptures taught them that true wisdom lay in the fear of God. So, as those people of Nazareth listened to Jesus their carpenter on that Sabbath day, what surprised them was this aspect of his teaching, a wisdom which demonstrated at once his great intellect, and his deep knowledge of God.

The answer to their questions, though hidden from them, should be clear to us. Jesus was the man who, above all men, was taught of the Holy Spirit, and the teaching had been absorbed, through all the hidden years, with a perfectly sinless and unclouded intelligence. It is out of man's sinful limitations that all the misinterpretation and misunderstanding of God's Word over the centuries have risen. Jesus had none of these limitations, and the Spirit who inspired the Scriptures was his teacher in them. The Gospels show how perfect his understanding in them was and demonstrate his great familiarity with them, as well as his ability to use them. No other ever used, or could use, the Word of God as he did.

There is another remarkable comment about him found in the Gospel of John. Visiting Jerusalem he taught in the Temple. This was a very different matter from preaching in the synagogue of Nazareth. All the religious scholarship of the day centred in this city. Here a false accent, a wrong emphasis, or a misquotation would be instantly spotted. But when Jesus came out of the villages of Galilee to the great city of his land, and opened his mouth to preach, surrounded by the most critical ears of his day, there was no hint of unfavourable reaction. On the contrary, 'The Jews were amazed and asked, "How did this man get such learning without having studied?"' (John 7:15).

The surprise of those Jerusalem scholars is all the more readily appreciated when we notice that the selfsame expression was used of the erudite Paul by Festus when he said, 'Your great learning is driving you insane' (Acts 26:24). It was this evidence of intellectual power that astonished the Jews. Here was one who had never studied in any of their great schools, and yet he had more than their schools could bestow. It is all too easy to pass over and miss the significance of Jesus' reply on this occasion. 'My teaching is not my own.

It comes from him who sent me.' The gifts of spiritual under-standing and authoritative utterance which amazed them — and every reader of the New Testament since — were the insignia of the Spirit's presence and teaching. The school in which Jesus had spent his time was unique. What the Jews witnessed in Jerusalem was the harvest of the hidden years of learning and obedience.

Two further tokens of the Spirit's presence in the growing Jesus may be mentioned. The first is from the Father at the Jordan baptism, 'This is my Son, whom I love; with him I am well pleased' (Matthew 3:17). That articulation of the divine pleasure referred, we may be sure, not merely to what had just taken place, but to the entire life which had gone before. Only now, after thirty years, had Jesus emerged out of obscurity into public view. But there was one eye, one heart, to which those years had been neither hidden nor obscure, the eye and the heart of the Father in heaven. They were years whose passing was marked with perfect obedience; and it was obedience embracing not merely the leading of the Spirit to manifest himself at this juncture, but the pressure of the Spirit to remain in obscurity through all the days until then.

According to the apostle we 'live and move and have our being' in God. Here was one man who delighted to do that and was conscious, as other men are not, that he did so. Near the end of his life he could declare, 'I always do what pleases him' (John 8:29). That was true, as the Father's testimony at Jordan makes clear, from the very beginning of his life on earth. For any man to please God he must, of course, live to the glory of God. Before man can do that, however, there must be not only inward purity, such as Jesus had from the moment of his conception, but also the positive energy of grace bringing each element of the soul into the harmony of a living, trusting, holy relationship with God. In other words, before man can please God, or live to his glory and honour, there must be a principle of spiritual, as well as of natural, life flowing in him. That principle is never operative apart from the presence and work of the Spirit. Through his presence and power it was always at work in Jesus.

41

The second of the two tokens is the statement of Jesus to John the Baptist assuring him that the baptism was necessary: 'It is proper for us to do this to fulfil all righteousness' (Matthew 3:15). It can be freely granted that these words reach out to and embrace all the later work of Jesus — his public ministry, death, and resurrection. But it must equally be stated that they reach back to the beginning as well. Jesus was, in fact, from the point of incarnation onwards, fulfilling 'all righteousness'. It would be wrong to isolate any part of his life, or his human experience, from the great saving work he came to accomplish. For that, only his entire, ongoing experience of living obedience to God would perfectly equip him. In order to accomplish that fulfilling of 'all righteousness', the human Jesus was always richly endowed with the Spirit. Of him it had been predicted long before, 'The Spirit of the LORD will rest on him — the Spirit of wisdom and of understanding, the Spirit of counsel and of power, the Spirit of knowledge . . . and he will delight in the fear of the LORD' (Isaiah 11:2,3). From birth right through to death, the daily life of Jesus fulfilled and unfolded that prophecy, and did so perfectly.

The Holy Spirit — and the family life

One area of those hidden years and the life of this Spirit-filled child about which interesting questions arise is the relationship between him, his mother, Joseph, and the rest of the household of which he was a part. With the appearance of the angel to Joseph in a dream and the message brought him about the girl he was to marry — 'what is conceived in her is from the Holy Spirit. She will give birth to a son, and you are to give him the name Jesus, because he will save his people from their sins' (Matthew 1:20,21) — there must have been a very special awareness from the outset that this son was to be a unique person. How did that affect the home?

Again, the appearance of the angel Gabriel to Mary, and the imparting of the same message of a unique conception and birth, with all its strange implications for her reputation, her womanhood, and her motherhood, must have been a completely overwhelming experience. One thing that must have helped steady her mind, and comfort her heart in her moments of perplexity, was the salutation of Gabriel to her with its great central assurance: 'The Lord is with you' (Luke 1:28). There is no doubt that both Joseph and Mary would identify those messages, and all the other divine events which overtook them, as pointing to the fact that this son would be the Messiah of Israel, that is, God's anointed Servant. How did they manage to cope with all this? How could they hope to live with and rear such a child?

In this connection there are issues which, again, underwrite the true humanity of the incarnate Son, and which indicate how natural, in the very best sense, a Spirit-filled life should appear to others. From the outset, Mary and Joseph had to contend with factors which stirred their wonder.

It is with the appearance of the shepherds at the time of his birth that we are given the first glimpse into the troubled thoughts that must, often, have trembled in Mary's mind, and caused her great anxiety about the future of her first-born child: 'But Mary treasured up all these things and pondered them in her heart' (Luke 2:19). Then again, when they took him to the Temple and he underwent the rite of circumcision (for he was 'born under law'), and the Spirit-filled Simeon proclaimed him as the Saviour for whom he had been waiting, she — and Joseph — 'marvelled at what was said about him' (Luke 2:33). She must have thrilled with awe, and perhaps fear also, when Simeon went on to say to her, 'And a sword will pierce your own soul too' (Luke 2:35).

In view of all these factors, Mary has sometimes been criticized for being slow to appreciate all that Jesus was and had come to do. At first glance, her reactions to him on some occasions do seem strangely lacking in perception. For example, she was to wonder at him lingering behind in the Temple among Israel's teachers, and was all too ready to rebuke: 'Son, why have you treated us like this?' (Luke 2:48); and at the first of his miracles her attitude called for his rebuke: 'My time has not yet come' (John 2:4). Afterwards, at the height of his activity and fame, loving fears about his welfare indicate that even then she failed to see his work in the fulness of its meaning (Mark 3:20,21,31-35).

We would tend to think, perhaps, that from the very beginning of his life, his mother of all people should have had a clear conception that he was truly the Son of God. Like so many other thoughts, we have only to think it when we see how emphatically wrong it is. The fact is, the story rings with truth when we realize how thoroughly human Joseph and Mary are in their restricted insight into the nature and calling of the child Jesus in spite of the special revelation they had.

This matter requires careful reflection. If the attitude of Joseph and Mary to Jesus had been other than it was, that would entail the denial of the truly human dimension in the experiences of our Lord as he grew. Not only did his mission require progressive development in his human consciousness, and actual, personal experience of temptations and sorrows — and he knew both — but Jesus could not in any real sense of the word have been 'obedient to them' (Luke 2:51) if the relationship had moved on a plane where Joseph and Mary had full understanding that he was God. Nor, supposing such knowledge, could they have watched and been thrilled as they saw the child grow in stature and wisdom, and in favour with God and with man. That knowledge would have shredded the bond of his humanity to their own and cut through all that bound him in real dependence, as a real child, to them and their care over him. This bears upon us also. He could not have become like his brothers, had he not been truly the virgin's son. His human experience would not be true incarnation had his humanity not been subject to all normal human conditions. Instead of being one with us, in all but our sins, he would have been as alien to us as 'Superman'. This principle enables us to see why the mystery of his real deity had to be shielded while he was on earth. Had it been otherwise, the thought of his divinity would have pushed his humanity, with its utter necessity for his mediatorial role, completely out of view.

In actual fact, it took three years of patient teaching and self-disclosure, as well as crucifixion and resurrection, to convince his disciples of his divine godhead and glory. Perhaps full, unencumbered awareness of this at any earlier point would have disqualified all of them for unembarrassed fellowship with him. Even his teaching and preaching as man among men — as well as the sign-significance of his miracles — would have been impossible had all immediately been aware of who he truly was. His hearers no doubt would have listened to him, and stood in trembling awe of him, but they could have had no sense of rapport, nor of any truly shared experience with him. There were things which could be revealed, fittingly, only when his redemptive accomplishment had been secured. True, there were intimations of his actual identity being given all along, and some who, like Anna and Simeon, were given eyes to see the truth at the very beginning, but those factors do not destroy, nor even detract from, the fundamental principle of his incarnation, that he was truly man — 'made like his brothers in every way' (Hebrews 2:17).

Such considerations as these should help us see that every event connected with the messianic manifestations of Jesus would come, even to his mother, as a fresh discovery and a new surprise. Each of those events as it took place would tend to stand isolated in her mind, and yet be consciously interpreted as a part of a wider whole which she could not readily, or perfectly, visualize. She knew the beginning, and she had some idea of the grand end-purpose. But she could not know all the route that led from the one to the other. Each step along it was a fresh revelation, a gradual unfolding, of the way she must walk. Only in this way could she truly, without any self-consciousness, as a mother and woman in the Israel of her day, fulfil all the rites of the law for herself and her child.

The Holy Spirit — and the witness of Simeon

The first of the obligatory rites in which the child had to participate was circumcision. This was the great token of submission to the law and acceptance, in its obligations and privileges, of the covenant between God and the seed of Abraham (see Genesis 17:10-12). The ceremony took place when he was eight days old and he was given the name Jesus (Jehovah the Saviour). This indicates the very intimate relation in which the incarnate Son stands to the old covenant. It reminds us that the entire revelation of the Old Testament was a preparation for his coming, and for the manifestation of God in him. Both circumcision and the purification customs which God had decreed should follow birth had direct reference to the sin in which each person is born, and the need of blood-shedding and blood sacrifice for its removal. When Jesus underwent those rites he did so, not because of any personal sin of his own, but as a sign and seal — as circumcision is described by Paul (Romans 4:11) — of acceptance of the obligations of his people. It was their redemption he had come to implement and it was necessary that he 'fulfil all righteousness' on their behalf.

It was when the time for 'their purification according to the Law of Moses had been completed' that Joseph took mother and child to Jerusalem, to 'present him to the Lord' in the Temple there (Luke 2:22). Purification, of course, involved sacrifice and in the case of Joseph and Mary it was the special sacrifice permitted for those who were poor — a pigeon in the place of a lamb.

It was on this occasion that Simeon, who had earlier been told by the Spirit of God that he 'would not die before he had seen the Lord's Christ' (Luke 2:26), spoke prophetically, uttering the message which caused Joseph and Mary solemn amazement (v. 33). His words about the universal design and significance of God's salvation purposes through the child must have impressed them afresh with his uniqueness. Even then, the full significance of his deity, or the events by which his work was to be accomplished, could not be known by them. Again and again, as his ministry unfolded before her, Mary wavers and becomes confused through human weakness. We have already noted Mark's record of his family's concern for him during his Galilean ministry.

The words of Simeon to Mary are very striking: 'This child is destined to cause the falling and rising of many in Israel, and to be a sign that will be spoken against, so that the thoughts of many hearts will be revealed. And a sword will pierce your own soul too' (Luke 2:34,35). Simeon had a solemn message not just for Mary, but for us today as well. Jesus cannot be side-stepped by anyone. Sooner or later, everyone must take up a position with regard to him, and must decide for him or against him. It is not an outward doing good, or a so-called good life, that counts before God, or shows the deepest inclination of any heart, or determines the salvation of any soul; what really matters is one's personal relationship to Christ.

There is, too, in the message of Simeon a testimony to Mary and Joseph — and succeeding ages — regarding the messianic status of Jesus. The Spirit is not only *in* the child, he is witnessing *about* him. This is a characteristic of the Spirit's witness to Christ. Its principle is unchangingly consistent. 'He will bring glory to me', said Jesus about the Spirit's ministry, 'by taking from what is mine and making it known to you' (John 16:14). That was taking place in the Temple for Joseph and Mary, through Simeon. At the same time it was through their ministry to him, and their care over him that 'the child grew and became strong'. God prepared the Saviour for the work he had come to do, in the school of true human experience.

4
The Self-understanding of Jesus

*'Why were you searching for me? . . . Didn't you
know I had to be in my Father's house?'* (Luke 2:49).

These words bring us the second real glimpse of Jesus which
we have during the first thirty years of his life. They are complementary to what we have learned already from the events
of his infancy, but add a broader dimension to that picture,
and teach us some further lessons of how he lived during the
hidden years. They are different from the words which we
looked at in the last chapter, for they are spoken not about
Jesus but by him. They are, in fact, the first recorded words
of Jesus which we have, and that gives them a special interest
for Christians.

They come from the account of Jesus in the Temple, when
he was twelve years of age. It is marvellous that we have
them, for they provide the single stepping-stone we have in his
progress from infancy to the opening of his public ministry,
when he was about thirty years of age. They afford some insight into the work of the Holy Spirit in the growing Jesus,
and how that contributed to the self-understanding of Jesus.
The Spirit's ministry was a major factor in the messianic self-
consciousness of Jesus, and these first recorded words indicate that, already, this element was the most potent, single
influence in his understanding of himself. The young Jesus
was already interpreting his life over against his knowledge
of, and obedience to, the Father's will and the mission that
the Father had given him to fulfil.

48

The Holy Spirit and Jesus' sense of obedience

One of the features which appear on the very surface of this narrative is the desire of this twelve-year-old Jesus to serve God the Father, to be about his business, and to yield him perfect obedience. The obedience to the divine will which is the chief characteristic of his entire life was, even at this stage of his human experience, so native to his mind and heart, that he expected it to be perfectly obvious to others also, and especially to Mary and Joseph.

For four days he had been out of sight of Mary and Joseph. For three days they had been worried and concerned — 'Son, why have you treated us like this? Your father and I have been anxiously searching for you' (Luke 2:48). Despite the anxiety of which Mary speaks, they evidently trusted him very deeply. They had not been over-anxious at all through the first day. The indication is that they regarded him as steady, obedient, and trustworthy even when he was out of their sight. This very reliability probably added to their concern as the days went by and there was no sign of him. But where did they find him at last? Not idling his time away, nor getting into mischief. He was not in vain or unprofitable company. They 'found him in the temple courts, sitting among the teachers, listening to them and asking them questions' (v.46).

This anxiety on the part of Mary and Joseph in no way contradicts what they knew about his being the Messiah. If anything, their genuine human uneasiness establishes some of the elements already noticed in their relationship with the boy Jesus. At most, it shows that they did not yet fully, or constantly, recognize that since he was in reality the Christ of God there was no need for them to be too concerned about his welfare. In common with most of the disciples, it seems that it was only after Jesus' resurrection and the outpouring of the Holy Spirit at Pentecost that Mary fully realized who her son was. Only then was she able to interpret in their true light the announcements of the angels, the supernatural conception and so forth.

The reply of Jesus to Mary has often been regarded as a reproof. This is to mistake its meaning. It is much more an utterance of amazement. The fact is that, understood in this way, his words show that he was not in the least uneasy himself although he had not seen Mary and Joseph for some days. His human consciousness had no suspicion that they were anxious about him. Devoted as he was to them, he was, nevertheless, and especially as he was growing older, exceptionally self-reliant and strong in his personality. He was clearly surprised that they did not know where to find him, or that they should be so anxiously looking for him. How was it — and this is the real point of his question — that when they missed him they had not immediately realized that he had to be busy in the Temple about the concerns of his Father; about the revelation, the knowledge, the redemption of grace, and the service of God? Harking back to Mary's phrase, 'Your father and I', Jesus refers to God in a very emphatic sense as his Father because God, and not Joseph, is his real Father.

What we have here is, in fact, the boy Jesus demonstrating that quality of obedience to the Father's will that is the fundamental characteristic and the ruling principle of his entire life. This is what sets him apart from all other men who have ever lived. The Spirit of God has been at work, enlightening, teaching, and strengthening him to love the Father with all the heart and soul and mind. One of the main ministries of the Spirit in his experience would be the revealing of the Father's will. It is over against such continual increase in knowledge of that will, that his obedience could be expanded and perfected at every juncture; not that it was ever imperfect, but it had to keep pace with his experience, and it did. There was a process of learning in the expansion of his perfect obedience.

This identifies the youthful Jesus very closely with messianic prophecy. Obedience is one of the leading Servant characteristics predicted of Messiah in the Old Testament and already, at twelve years of age, it is manifesting itself in the strongest possible way. So clearly is this aspect of his life developing by this time, that he reminds no less a person than the woman who, after the flesh, was his mother, that he has a Father in heaven and this Father's work demands, always, his first attention. He was letting her know where his priorities lay, and the context in which he was doing so supports the view that he knew she would understand perfectly.

The Holy Spirit and Jesus' sense of sinlessness

Even this early, it would appear that not only was Jesus conscious of the very special relationship in which he stood to the Father personally, but that he realized that he stood in a special relationship to him morally and spiritually as well. Obedience to God is the most important thing for him already.

Again this is something which demands attention. Experience tells us how easily we become aware of failure or sinfulness. This must, by analogy, be true of the opposite moral qualities, of purity and sinlessness; conscience either accuses and condemns, or it clears and approves. In this connection, it is beyond doubt that Jesus knew he was free from sin. Two factors illustrate this.

Where sin was concerned, it is obvious that Jesus had a very tender conscience. One facet of his teaching which has deeply influenced the moral history of the world, was his insistence that it is the motive, or intention, behind any act that makes it sinful. While outward actions, deeds, and words contrary to God's law are sinful, they all proceed from within and are the effects of man's evil heart and inward sinfulness. Unlike the world of today, Jesus never ignored the root cause of all the misery of men, and the chief thrust of his moral and spiritual teaching emphasizes the *sinfulness* of sin. To his keen eye the world of men was lost in sin.

It is because of this that we find another doctrine, strongly and urgently asserted by Jesus. Man must have a radical change of nature; he must be renewed by the Holy Spirit; he must be born again. Such is the sin of all men, their inward inability to obey God, or amend their own ways, that this particular need admits of no exceptions (John 3:3). Every man, in every place and every time, must be regenerated in order to believe and be saved. All this means that Jesus, always, was very deeply conscious of the sin and need of all men. That is the first thing to note.

51

Secondly, in his eyes one of the most evil and dangerous traits of the human heart was to conceal or deny sin. Men must repent, that is, turn from their sin to God. Repentance must always include confession. The true turning in repentance was to be undertaken with frank confession of *being* wrong, as well as of *doing* wrong. To summarize, his teaching encouraged sinners to approach God with this prayer, 'God, have mercy on me, a sinner' (Luke 18:13).

Some of his strongest and most scathing remarks were directed against this particular aspect of man's sin. He invariably lashed at the hypocrisy, the self-satisfaction, and the self-adulation that went with it. It is what, again and again, stirred his anger against the Pharisees, with their outward righteousness and their inward corruption; their readiness to condemn others and approve themselves. This was what called from him his strongest condemnation of them: 'You are the ones who justify yourselves in the eyes of men, but God knows your hearts. What is highly valued among men is detestable in God's sight' (Luke 16:15).

It is this same Jesus, to whom the crowning sin in those men was actually the denial of sin, who says of himself and his relationship to the Father, 'I always do what pleases him' (John 8:29). He obviously believed himself to be free from sin. Although this consciousness may shine out more clearly in his teaching as he nears the end of his ministry, it is there from the very beginning.

The young boy knew that he had never forfeited his Father's love or his Father's approval. He is consciously engaged in the Father's business there in the Temple with the teachers of God's law, and it was genuinely human, and perhaps even childlike, that under the circumstances he had never thought that Mary and Joseph would be anxious. But when they came to fetch him, he went with them freely, without protest, to Nazareth and was 'obedient to them', for this also was the will of his heavenly Father.

At the outset of his ministry the first public act of obedience was baptism. John shrank from the task. He felt it was wrong, and that he required to be baptized by Jesus. That is a tremendously strong, because wholly unself-conscious, personal testimony to the sinlessness of Jesus. In turn Jesus accepts, in a calm, straightforward way John's testimony as being in absolute accord with the facts. He confirmed to John that his feeling, his impulse, was right (Matthew 3:14 ff). This is perfectly consistent with the fact that, unlike Paul, Jesus never confessed any sense of insufficiency for the task laid on him. Nor did he ever know anything of the need of God's forgiveness. All other men were to seek, and live by, mercy, but he did not require it. He never praised God for the undeserved compassion bestowed upon him, as Paul so frequently did.

This consciousness of his sinlessness goes even further, culminating in two unreserved claims which he made again and again. By his own utterances he stands over against all men as the only Saviour and the ultimate Judge. How could he have presented himself as such if there was the slightest burden on his conscience? Only because he knew that he himself was in no need of a Saviour could he know, and teach, that he was the Saviour who 'came to seek and to save what was lost' (Luke 19:10). He taught that all men would stand before him — 'The Son of Man' — in final judgement (Matthew 13:41; 25:31-33, etc.), and yet earnestly warned his disciples against rashly judging others in case their judgements recoiled on their own heads — 'Do not judge, or you too will be judged' (Matthew 7:1). All this in face of the fact that he himself assessed the spiritual state of other men without hesitation whenever occasion called for it.

At the end, this sinless self-consciousness endured even the fiery trial of desertion and death. As the shadows of the cross came upon him and he measured his own obedience, his conscience did not reproach him. The opposite was true. He looked up to the Father and said, 'I have brought you glory on earth by completing the work you gave me to do' (John 17:4). In Israel a man hanged on a tree was, by divine statute, cursed of God (Deuteronomy 21:23), and that alone would have given any God-fearing man cause for self-examination. But all the way to the cross, and even on the cross, the willing obedience of Jesus was without hesitation. It was obedience ever fortified by this knowledge of his own sinlessness. In the prospect, as well as the hour, of death, most men know that they have nothing with which to ransom their own souls. This man was so entirely free of guilt that he could say that he had actually come 'to give his life as a ransom for many' (Matthew 20:28).

The Holy Spirit and Jesus' sense of Sonship

In the time of Jesus, one of the titles commonly used for the Messiah was 'Son of God'. For example, at the trial of Jesus the high priest said to him, 'I charge you under oath by the living God: Tell us if you are the Christ, the Son of God' (Matthew 26:63). To which Jesus answered, 'Yes, it is as you say' (v.64). Here it is worth noting the inferences attaching to Jesus' use and acknowledgement of this special messianic title 'Son of God'. Sonship, of course, always implies and involves 'Fatherhood', and it is this Father/Son relationship, in its very deepest meaning, which most clearly unveils to us the self-estimate of Jesus,and his own interpretation of his relationship to God. That it was the great groundwork and foundation of all his thinking and teaching appears not so much in his use of the title 'Son', but rather in that of 'Father'. The former he used only infrequently, but the latter almost invariably when he spoke of his relationship to God. Implicit in this continual usage, as well as explicit in his teaching, is the truth that God was Father to Jesus in a way in which he was not Father to other men: 'I am returning to my Father and your Father, to my God and your God' (John 20:17).

However, when Jesus did use this title, Son, he did so in a very instructive way, for he used it to point men not only towards, but beyond, his messianic mission. For example, he uses the name to emphasize not only the mystery attaching to the being of God, but the mystery of his own essential being as well. 'No one knows the Son except the Father, and no one knows the Father except the Son and those to whom the Son chooses to reveal him' (Matthew 11:27). In other words, Father and Son are both alike a mystery. No man can see into that inner unity, nor know the Father personally, but by the revelation of the Son.

The unity implied here moves in the realm of personal relationship and mutual understanding, of communion and intimate knowledge. To the Father, Jesus is supremely and uniquely 'Son', and to Jesus, God is supremely and uniquely 'Father'. That is to say, only Jesus and God the Father stand thus related to one another. This 'Fatherhood' and this 'Sonship' are unique and confined to this relationship. Both differ from all others in their essential being, in that it involves a unity unknown elsewhere. It is their unity of being which explains their full, mutual understanding. They are in no sense a mystery to each other; instead, they know each other fully; nothing in the one is hidden from the other. What Jesus claims here is a supernatural, divine consciousness, for only if that is really present is he a mysterious being who can be known only by God. The other side of the equation applies in the same way; only because Jesus is God, can he know the Father in this unique way. This is a clear claim to deity. It is a revelation of his own deep, positive sense of divine Sonship.

Another occasion on which this consciousness of divine Sonship comes into the forefront of his teaching, also brings in the person of the Holy Spirit very directly. Jesus compares speaking against himself with speaking against the Spirit. In the context he is speaking very solemnly and specifically about the sin of blasphemy. It is clear that, in his thinking, this sin can be committed against himself as well as against the Holy Spirit. 'Anyone who speaks a word against the Son of Man will be forgiven, but anyone who speaks against the Holy Spirit will not be forgiven' (Matthew 12:32). Just as he has put himself upon a level with the Father, so he puts himself upon the same level as the Spirit.

One question that has often been aired is when this awareness of his being the Son had its origin in his experience, and various answers have been given. In fact, it was without beginning. We must not confuse the understanding the disciples had of him at first with his own self-consciousness. The disciples may have seen in him, initially, only a man anointed with the Spirit of God, but Jesus' own thinking never moved within those limits. The twelve-year-old child used the same word, 'my Father', as the dying Jesus on the cross, 'Father, forgive them'. The use of the title on this early visit to the Temple is just the first glimpse given us of his unique self-estimate. But it would be a complete mistake to suppose that this was the moment when that consciousness was born. Through the ministry of the Holy Spirit the child Jesus, as soon as he became aware of himself, recognized himself as the Son. The assurance belonged to him, not just in the high, crisis hours of his human experience, but all the journey through. Even at the end, it is not dimmed but shines with a clear radiance still; 'I tell you the truth, today you will be with me in paradise . . . Father, into your hands I commit my spirit' (Luke 23:43,46). It was without end, as it had been without beginning.

The Holy Spirit and Jesus' sense of messiahship

One of the characteristics of the life of Jesus is his sense of purpose. He knew he had been given a unique calling and that calling dominated his life. We hear echoes of it in almost all his teaching about himself. The formula varies, but the meaning is always the same: 'For this very reason I came to this hour' (John 12:27), 'For this reason I was born', 'For this I came into the world' (John 18:37). This sense of calling he interpreted in terms of the Messiah promised in the Old Testament Scriptures.

It is this conception of himself that is involved in the words at the head of this chapter. It is certain that when he came out into public ministry, some seventeen or more years after this occasion, his sense of messiahship was fully clear to him. That is implicit in his words to the Baptist, 'Let it be so now; it is proper for us to do this to fulfil all righteousness' (Matthew 3:15).

That this was uppermost in his understanding of his work is quite clear in another transaction which took place between himself and the Baptist. John was languishing in prison. His faith in Jesus as the Christ seems to have come under severe testing, and in this extremity he sent to Jesus the query, 'Are you the one who was to come, or should we expect someone else?' (Matthew 11:3). The answer of Jesus, like the question itself, was couched in terms of messianic prophecy — of the blind receiving their sight, the lame being made to walk, the deaf hearing, and the gospel being proclaimed to the poor. When the essence of that was reported back to John he must have been greatly reassured, and had his faith reaffirmed.

The importance of this for us lies in what Jesus went on to say to the crowd about John the Baptist. 'This is the one about whom it is written: "I will send my messenger ahead of you, who will prepare your way before you"' (Matthew 11:10). Thus Jesus affirmed that John was the promised prophet, who coming as an Elijah, would be the 'forerunner' of Messiah. Jesus sealed that thought on the hearts of his hearers by quoting the messianic prophecy of Malachi 3:1. From such usage it is abundantly clear that Jesus regarded himself as the promised Messiah, and John as the great prophet who was to introduce Messiah's ministry.

The Jewish world of that day had formed its own very definite picture of what Messiah would be like and what he would accomplish. Messiah was longed for by most Jews of the time, so that in his kingly glory he would free them from the domination of the Roman conquerors. Prophetic writings were being interpreted — or rather, misinterpreted — to suit the particular hour. This is one reason why Jesus refrained from openly proclaiming his messianic mission to the crowds and unveiled it, even to the disciples, only slowly and, most frequently, in the form of parable.

For the Jews the cross seemed the denial of any messianic characteristics that they had seen in Jesus. That was because they had never rightly understood the great prophetic passages — such as Psalm 22, or Isaiah 53 — in their literal, personal, messianic meaning and application. Yet those very passages must have informed the understanding of Jesus himself, and of John the Baptist in his preaching of Jesus as the Lamb provided by God for the sin of the world.

It is of this particular aspect of his messianic awareness that

B.B. Warfield speaks in a powerful passage on the progress of Jesus to the cross: 'Every suggestion of escape from it by the use of his intrinsic divine powers, whether of omnipotence or of omniscience, was treated by him first and last as a temptation of the evil one. The death in which his life ends is conceived, therefore, as the goal in which his life culminates. He came into the world to die, and every stage of the road that led up to this issue was determined not for him, but by him: he was never the victim but always the Master of circumstance, and pursued his pathway from beginning to end, not merely in full knowledge from the start of all its turns and twists up to its bitter conclusion, but in complete control both of them and it. His life of humiliation, sinking into his terrible death, was therefore not his misfortune, but his achievement as the promised Messiah, by and in whom the kingdom of God is to be established in the world: it was the work which as Messiah he came to do' (B.B. Warfield, *Works*, Baker Book House Company, 1981, vol.3, p.161).

The Holy Spirit and Jesus' sense of uniqueness

Very little can be known about the nature of self-awareness and self-consciousness in any man. It defies all attempts to analyse or explain it and yet every person with normal human faculties knows what it is. It is in this realm particularly, that Scripture attributes what we are rationally and morally to the ministry of the Holy Spirit. That is helpful. If Scripture teaches us that the gifts, the faculties, the graces of ordinary men are given and exercised in harmony with the power of the Spirit, then it pinpoints the area where the Spirit's work must be traced in this extraordinary person, Jesus the Christ. By analogy we can see that it was the Spirit's function to endow the human nature of the Lord Jesus with all the normal human faculties, gifts, and graces to make him true and perfect man. It was the Spirit's function too, to quicken those gifts and graces and bring them into their full exercise as he pursues his redemptive ministry to its ultimate goal.

In the Gospel of John we are told that, 'to him God gives the Spirit without limit' (John 3:34). John the Baptist preached that Jesus would, out of his own unmeasured unction of the Spirit's power, baptize his followers also: 'The man on whom you see the Spirit come down and remain is he who will baptise with the Holy Spirit' (John 1:33). Jesus himself, at the height of his ministry, taught the same truth: '"Whoever believes in me, as the Scripture has said, streams of living water will flow from within him." By this he meant the Spirit, whom those who believed in him were later to receive' (John 7:38,39). The Lord Jesus then, is a man who was able, always, to experience being 'filled to the measure of all the fulness of God' (Ephesians 3:19). Of Jesus Paul specifically taught, 'For God was pleased to have all his fulness dwell in him' (Colossians 1:19), and that dwelling was by the Spirit and from the moment of incarnation.

On this matter, one of the Scottish theologians of last century makes some observations which are very helpful. 'The Spirit was given to Him, in consequence of the personal union, in a measure which no mere man could possess, constituting the link between the Deity and humanity, perpetually imparting the full consciousness of His personality, and making Him inwardly aware of His divine Sonship at all times' (George Smeaton, *The Doctrine of the Holy Spirit*, Banner of Truth, 1961, p. 126). Of particular importance in that excerpt is the observation that it is the Holy Spirit who constitutes the 'link between the Deity and humanity' of Christ. Dr Smeaton clarifies this by saying: 'It was the Holy Spirit that formed His human nature and directed the tenor of His earthly life. His human nature had no distinct personality, nor any self-directing principle, apart from the personal union; . . . *The communication from the one nature to the other was by the Spirit* [Smeaton's own italics] . . . The Godhead dwelling in Him made all due communications to His manhood by the Holy Ghost . . . Nothing was undertaken but by the Spirit's direction; nothing spoken but by His guidance; nothing executed but by His power.' It is a matter of great regret that such a brilliant theologian does not elaborate more fully on this theme which he could have handled so informatively.

This theological understanding of the incarnate Son is finely and cogently articulated in the writings of another Scottish theologian of last century, Dr Hugh Martin. Emphasizing the true humanity of the Lord Jesus he writes, 'The second person of Godhead, humbling himself in human flesh, did not draw directly on his own divine resources, but suffering his humanity to feel all its own insufficiency as a weak, dependent creature, he drew all his strength from God through the Spirit' (Hugh Martin, *The Abiding Presence*, Edinburgh, Knox Press, p.104). In another connection, Dr Martin reiterates the same sentiment with considerable emphasis: 'So far as Christ's obedience unto death is concerned, he places in abeyance for a time, and by Covenant agreement, his right to draw on the resources of his own Godhead any otherwise than as a man, an obedient servant and a believing son may do' (p.103). He adds this telling comment: 'The fundamental idea of his humiliation is not apprehended unless this be understood.'

Abraham Kuyper, the famous Dutch theologian of last century writes along the same lines. He says, 'In his conception and birth, the Holy Spirit effected, not only a separation from sin, but also endowed his human nature with the glorious gifts, powers, and faculties of which that human nature was susceptible. Hence his human nature received these gifts and powers, not from the Son by communication from the divine nature, but from the Holy Spirit by communication to the human nature. And this', adds Kuyper, 'should be thoroughly understood' (*The Work of the Holy Spirit*, pp.94,95).

It is apparent that the Spirit not only endowed Jesus with the rich gifts of which these men speak but supervised their gradual entry into full activity as he grew from childhood to manhood. This was an ongoing process, a succession that was coincident with the passing days and years of his humiliation. The knowledge of the child Jesus, for example, was not as advanced nor as full as the knowledge of the man Jesus. Thus he learned as his stay on earth deepened his human experience.

The thrust of this chapter has been to remind us how truly human the incarnate Son was. The Saviour held out in the overtures of the gospel is truly God. But he is also truly man, and as such, has come very close to us. He became man in order that he could suffer and die for our sins. He took our nature in order that he could bear the guilt of our sins. 'Since the children have flesh and blood, he too shared in their humanity so that by his death he might destroy him who holds the power of death — that is, the devil . . . For this reason he had to be made like his brothers in every way, in order that he might become a merciful and faithful high priest in service to God, and that he might make atonement for the sins of the people' (Hebrews 2: 14-17).

5
The Baptism of Jesus

'As soon as Jesus was baptised, he went up out of the water. At that moment heaven was opened, and he saw the Spirit of God descending like a dove and lighting on him. And a voice from heaven said, "This is my Son, whom I love; with him I am well pleased"' (Matthew 3:16,17).

Here we have the account of our Lord Jesus Christ's baptism. The hidden years are being left behind and this is the first step of his public ministry. Interestingly, when the Jewish priests took up their office they underwent a type of baptismal, or ceremonial, washing; 'Then bring Aaron and his sons to the entrance to the Tent of Meeting and wash them with water' (Exodus 29:4). When our great High Priest begins the work which he came into the world to accomplish he seeks the washing of public baptism.

This public appearance of Jesus is the first information the Gospels give of him since the Temple visit when he was twelve. There, as we have seen, two things stood out for him, sharpening his awareness of who he was and of what he had come to accomplish: the Temple was his Father's house, and the work of the Father his life-mission. In that conviction he returned to Nazareth, and in willing submission to Joseph and Mary fulfilled all righteousness. Those years of which so little is known were characterized by obedience to God and are enfolded in the approval voiced from heaven, 'with him I am well pleased'. The burning consciousness of his mission must often have tested patience, but the *how* and the *when* he left unasked and unanswered. In the patient obedience of these years is seen the signature of his perfection and sinlessness.

It is with this emergence of Jesus from the years of obscurity that our subject comes out into the light of revelation once more. With his reappearance, we have the next occasion on which we can consider the ministry of the Holy Spirit in his life. It has been stressed that the Holy Spirit never claims the limelight in his work. His task is to point always to the Saviour. His office, in relation to Christ, is to glorify him in the eyes of sinners. Yet, enough is revealed to make clear the importance of that ministry to the Mediator. We are shown in a variety of ways that the man Christ Jesus was not expected to carry through the work of the Messiah without the continual operation and powerful leading of the Holy Spirit. It was in the Spirit's anointing power that his human nature was to be the perfect instrument of the Son of God for his wonderful work. However, this must not detract from the doctrine of Christ as the complete Saviour. The Holy Spirit is the Sanctifier but not the Saviour of God's people. He was not incarnate, he did not suffer, he did not die for our sins. Let the words of the *Westminster Shorter Catechism* sound in our hearts again and again: 'The only Redeemer of God's elect is the Lord Jesus Christ.'

At the baptism of the Lord Jesus we have a further glimpse of our subject. This is one of the 'mountain peak' or 'crisis' experiences in the life of the Saviour. In them the veil is briefly, lightly, lifted and we have the clearest views of the Spirit's presence and work in the person of the Saviour.

John the Baptist and his messianic witness

From earliest times questions have been raised as to why Jesus went to be baptized. But there are good reasons for this baptism and we must probe them a little.

The first thing to notice is that the difficulty was actually felt and voiced before the baptism took place at all. We read, 'But John was trying to prevent him' (v.14). John was shocked at the very thought of baptizing Jesus and protested his sense of shock. John and Jesus were related and there is every evidence that John's mother, Elizabeth, was very well-informed about who Mary's first-born son was, and thought of him in the loftiest terms as 'my Lord' (Luke 1:42,43). The very fact that the Baptist protests indicates that he regarded him highly and already had strong reasons for suspecting that he was the Messiah. This has been queried because of the subsequent statement by John, 'I myself did not know him' (John 1:31). This has all too often been taken to mean that they were strangers to each other. In view of their relationship, their nearness in age, and the way Jewish people cherished family connections, this is hardly the most acceptable explanation of what John meant.

When John made that statement he went on to say something which clarifies what he did mean. He reveals that, before the baptism of Jesus, the Spirit had said: 'The man on whom you see the Spirit come down and remain is he who will baptise with the Holy Spirit' (John 1:33). In other words, the key to interpret John's statement lies alongside it. He had in mind a knowledge higher than ordinary day-to-day acquaintance. He was saying that it had not been disclosed to him, even though he was the messianic forerunner, that Jesus of Nazareth was actually the one he was to introduce and authenticate as Messiah.

In his attempt to ward off Jesus' participation in the baptism of repentance, John, reasoning that the lesser must be blessed of the greater (cf. Hebrews 7:7), expressed his feeling of needing to be baptized by Jesus. It is quite clear that Jesus accepted this inference as valid, and his doing so is one more evidence of his strong, inward, messianic self-consciousness. This was his experience even before his baptism or the ratification which accompanied it. 'Jesus replied, "Let it be so now; it is proper for us to do this to fulfil all righteousness." Then John consented' (Matthew 3:15). It is this insistence of Jesus that compels us to look for the real reason why he should be baptized with a baptism that spoke of sin and the need of cleansing.

The significance of Christ's baptism

Only when we appreciate *why* the Lord not only submitted to baptism but insistently sought it, will we be able to understand its deep, abiding, spiritual significance. The question *why* has a sharp edge to it because the baptism of John was undoubtedly a baptism of repentance, a baptism for sinners. It is this factor, and fear of its possible threat to his full deity, which has evoked all sorts of strange theories down the years to explain its occurrence. These range from a denial of the baptism altogether, right through to the more radical view that it suggests the intrinsic sinfulness of Jesus. The answer lies, not in denying the baptism, or the fact that it referred to sin and repentance, but in the actual nature of Jesus' mission. We must look for it along the twin lines of his true humiliation, and his complete identification with his people as their representative and substitute.

Understanding the meaning of baptism according to the scriptural teaching will help us answer the question. What is the fundamental idea, the basic ground-thought, attaching to biblical baptism? While Christian believers differ in their understanding about the mode and subjects of baptism, most would find common ground in accepting that baptism, in one way or another, represents identification or union with some person, group, or thing. In the case of Christian baptism, of course, it is identification or union with Jesus Christ.

That concept of union and close identity between himself and his brothers was often in the mind of Jesus, and stands in the forefront of his teaching. It is given memorable illustration by him, for example, in the parable of the vine and the branches: 'I am the vine; you are the branches' (John 15:5). That picture of actual union and harmony is very familiar to all Christians. The fundamental thought is that of engrafting. It cannot be mistaken, and if we carry the thought of engrafting over into the sacrament we touch the very heart of the scriptural doctrine of baptism.

The apostle Paul provides a key which we can use to unlock the meaning of baptism. He casts light on the closeness with which the believer is bound to Christ and to all other believers in Christ. He has just been speaking about the work of the Spirit in believers, and especially about the distribution of various gifts, and he says, 'All these are the work of one and the same Spirit, and he gives them to each man, just as he determines. The body is a unit, though it is made up of many parts; and though all its parts are many, they form one body. So it is with Christ. For we were all baptised by one Spirit into one body' (1 Corinthians 12:11-13).

Paul is thinking about three specific things here. Firstly, the diversity that is to be found among Christians when it comes to gifts, abilities, and callings. Secondly, he is stressing that, despite this variation in gifts, in Christ believers have an intimate bond of union which surmounts such differences. This bond is so close that he uses the human body as the analogy that best illustrates it — legs, hands, feet; they all differ and they all have their own function, but essentially they are one. They are one for the very simple, basic reason that they are part of the same body. Finally, he points to the regenerating work of the Spirit as proof of believers all being one in Christ.

It should be clear that Paul is writing about inward, and not merely outward baptism. It is the heart-renewal of the Spirit, for only that links its subjects into newness and oneness of life in Christ. But the important thing for us to notice from this passage is the thought that baptism unites and identifies and engrafts. When it is the baptism of the Spirit — his powerful, renewing, regenerating work in the soul of man, then there is powerful spiritual bonding. When it is the water baptism that symbolizes this spiritual work, then the dominant, leading idea and ground-thought is still that of union and engrafting and oneness. In water baptism we have the powerful symbol — the outward sign and seal — of the inward spiritual work. So the thought of bonding or engrafting enshrines the theology and the doctrinal significance of baptism.

The fundamental idea in baptism then — irrespective of the other questions about it which divide believers — is union with Christ. That carries with it union in the mystical body of Christ, the church of which he is King and Head. The essential message at the heart of biblical baptism is beautifully simple; 'The members are many, the body is one.'

The *Shorter Catechism* penetrates deeply into the core of the matter. It says: 'Baptism is a sacrament, wherein the washing with water in the name of the Father, and of the Son, and of the Holy Ghost, doth signify and seal our ingrafting into Christ, and partaking of the benefits of the covenant of grace, and our engagement to be the Lord's.'

Notice the threefold exposition it gives of the significance of baptism. Baptism stands for intimate union with Christ. It signifies and seals 'our ingrafting into Christ'. The second thing is this, our 'partaking of the benefits of the covenant of grace'. True, spiritual baptism, the reality which water baptism represents, puts us into possession of all that Christ bestows as Mediator of the covenant. The third thing that baptism stands for is 'our engagement to be the Lord's'. That expresses the powerful self-commitment that grace works in the heart of a believer. All that we are is given over to be Christ's. Those basic ideas about what baptism means will interpret for us the meaning of Christ's baptism.

At Jordan, we have the great Head of the church seeking and submitting himself to baptism. What is the leading thought in baptism when the baptism concerned is the baptism, not of one of the members but the actual Head of the body, Christ himself? What can this baptism mean and signify? Unless the fundamental doctrine is to change and baptism is to become something essentially other than it normally is, it must mean the same in this baptism as in any other specific instance.

The elements which actually define the meaning of any doctrine are not subject to change. If some one element is so deeply embedded in the nature of baptism as to constitute its essence, that element will always characterize it. It follows that if the doctrine of baptism, in its key meaning, does not change, the benefits and realities symbolized do not change either. Those must remain the same irrespective of other circumstances if words are not to change their meaning capriciously.

Is it possible that this can be so? Can baptism have essentially the same meaning for Christ as it has for the Christian believer? Can the key which opens up its meaning for us help us in this particular instance? It is necessary, of course, to safeguard our thinking about the Lord Jesus. A baptism of repentance does not imply any sin in him. Yet sin was, after all, bringing him into these very circumstances; not his own sin, but ours.

Scriptural evidence excludes any such notion that his baptism indicates personal sin in our Lord. It also excludes the idea that baptism effects any inward renewal or regeneration. Indeed, doctrinal considerations as to the nature of Christ's baptism exclude completely any notion of baptismal regeneration. They confirm it as an unscriptural idea which has filtered down, not from the New Testament, but from late second century controversies. To identify baptism and regeneration — as is still done in many quarters — is to confuse the symbol, the washing with water, with the reality symbolized, the inward regeneration and renewal of the sinner. The fact that Christ was baptized should in itself have precluded this confusion of two different things, and pointed up how alien to the New Testament teaching baptismal regeneration really is. It can certainly have no place in the baptism of the sinless Jesus, and that should have alerted men to the fact that it should have no place in the baptism which is so closely analogous to it. To clarify our thinking on this issue is to safeguard our doctrine of baptism also.

According to the Catechism, baptism 'doth signify and seal our ingrafting into Christ'. Can it be so in this case? The answer is yes. It symbolizes his engrafting of the church to himself; his public acknowledgement of the union; his unashamed identification with its members before God and man. This is the Saviour, the King and Head of the church identifying himself, openly, publicly, officially, with every last individual in the church.

Baptism is the public inauguration of his ministry. The first thing he does is to declare, in this symbolical way, his solidarity with his own people. He was adopting into union with

68

himself, freely and voluntarily, the people he had come to save — the great, numberless multitude who make up the redeemed. He has come where they are — far off, lost, separated from God by sin and sin's guilt. Christ has come as their great representative — as the last Adam — to work for them, and stand with them, and bring them back to God.

Here is Christ, entering into open, public identification with them. In baptism he is engaging to be theirs, and covenanting to them all the benefits of the covenant of grace. He is undertaking to be their Redeemer. He is contracting to be their mediatorial representative before God and his holy throne. Publicly and officially, spiritually and sacramentally, Jesus of Nazareth is to bear all the responsibilities, all the obligations, all the debts, all the sins and guilt of all the elect people of God. He is engaging, to put it very simply, to be their Saviour.

From now on he is in open, confessed union with them before the Father and the watching world. Without him, the Head, the body does not, cannot, exist. He is their representative and he is to be their substitute, and he is the one because he is first of all the other — that is, he is their substitute *because* he is their representative. The deep implication of all this is his covenanting himself into union with us. The obligations he was taking up included payment of sin's debt to righteousness and holiness, to God the Judge of all.

At this stage we must pause for serious reflection. The thought of Christ's taking our place must condemn any sin in our lives else that sin will rise in condemnation against us. To feel sin condemned in us and condemning our life is the first step in realizing our need of the same Saviour whom we view at Jordan. His baptism there led on to, and ensured another baptism — the baptism of blood on the cross. This is no idle, speculative theology. This is the Son of God incarnate, dealing with us, and dealing for us, and equipping himself to save sinners to the everlasting praise of God's name. The factors with which we are dealing here are to be estimated and weighed in terms of ultimate reality. They represent the most deeply significant events this world has ever known. They are the truths against which we have, in the final analysis, to weigh our own hearts and value our own lives.

The Spirit filling and baptizing Jesus

The biblical narrative does not allow us to overlook at this place, any more than in others, the twofold aspect inherent in baptism. There is an outward and an inward side to true baptism. Therefore its very nature makes us anticipate, even at Jordan, a work which only the divine power of the Spirit can accomplish. When we look for his presence it is immediately apparent. 'Heaven was opened, and he saw the Spirit of God descending like a dove and lighting on him.' There is not merely the outward and tangible, the objective participation in water baptism, but there is also an inward filling by the Spirit of God, a subjective experience of the Spirit's anointing power.

At this critically important juncture in the life of Jesus, the outset of his public ministry, this presence and filling of the Spirit must have been enormously comforting and reassuring to his heart. The Spirit is here as the executor of the divine purposes and in that capacity he is setting the divine seal, and the divine approval, upon what has just taken place. He is ratifying and sealing the engrafting of the Head into union with all his members, the church. His seal, given publicly and openly before God and before men, identifies and ratifies Jesus of Nazareth as the Messiah of God. He is the Anointed One spoken of in the many predictive messianic prophecies.

The anointing of Jesus with the fulness, the power, the grace of the Holy Spirit will impart to him all the tenderness and strength of love, which personal union with his church is going to demand and require of his human nature. The Holy Spirit is anointing and filling a nature which, although in personal union with the eternal Son of God, is still a true — therefore weak and creaturely — human nature. Significantly, he comes in the semblance of a dove. It was the dove who returned to the ark with the olive branch, a token of the receding of the flood, and of the return of conditions of peace and blessing to the earth which had experienced solemn, dreadful, judgement. Here, too, the coming of the Spirit as a dove signalled peace replacing judgement.

There is a significant difference when the Holy Spirit came down upon the church at Pentecost. Then he came as the Spirit of fire and burning. This is how it is put: 'Suddenly a sound like the blowing of a violent wind came from heaven and filled the whole house where they were sitting. They saw what seemed to be tongues of fire that separated and came to rest on each of them. All of them were filled with the Holy Spirit' (Acts 2:2-4). In fact, the Spirit is frequently portrayed in Scripture as a fire or in terms of burning.

John the Baptist himself actually spoke of the Lord Jesus baptizing men with 'the Holy Spirit and with fire' (Matthew 3:11). Why, then, did the Spirit not come upon Jesus himself in this dramatic and searching way? The answer is to be found simply along the lines of the scriptural teaching on the sinless nature of our Lord's humanity. Fire symbolizes the purging element of the Spirit's work, the burning up and the burning out of the dross of sin. But this man, even when he stands so intimately identified with sinners as he now does — engrafted into union with them — is not a partaker in their sin, and so there is nothing in him to be burned out, or purged away by the fire of the Spirit.

It is to be observed that the Spirit actually descended out of an opened heaven. Matthew calls special attention to it. The Greek actually says, 'look' or 'behold'. This was not merely a subjective experience in the mind of Jesus. It was definitely a miracle, occurring in full view of all who were present there with John and Jesus. There is no doubt that this was partially a testimony to Jesus himself, intended, as George Smeaton says, 'to confirm and encourage the Lord Jesus before entering on His arduous work' (*Doctrine of the Holy Spirit*, p.127). It is Luke who mentions that it was while Jesus was praying to the Father that this opening of heaven took place (Luke 3:21). On subsequent occasions, during important moments in his ministry, Jesus is spoken of as seeking the Father in prayer. In fact, it should encourage us that Jesus was, very certainly and truly, a man of prayer. There is nothing at all incongruous in this. It is one more indicator of how truly man he was.

The Bible only very occasionally speaks of heaven being opened. It happened in the experience of Ezekiel (Ezekiel 1:1); of Stephen, the first martyr of the New Testament church (Acts 7:56); and of John on Patmos (Revelation 4:1). The Spirit who came down evidently remained on Jesus for some time in that visible form. The Baptist mentions this abiding or resting (John 1:32,33) of the Spirit on the Lord quite specifically and it is surely to remind his hearers that *he* knew and could testify that Jesus was the predicted Messiah.

The approval of the Father

Smeaton remarks on the fact that all three persons of the Godhead were involved in this anointing which took place out of the opened heaven. He says, 'The anointer was the Father, the anointed was the Son, the unction, or anointing oil (Psalm 45:7) was the Holy Ghost, a divine Person of equal rank' (*Doctrine of the Holy Spirit*, p.127).

This filling and anointing of Jesus does not, of course, mean that he was not formerly full of the Spirit. We have seen that he was. But this fulness indicates that he had now been equipped by the Holy Spirit with all *official* gifts needed to begin his open ministry as Messiah. At the time of his conception it was a matter of the forming, and then later, of the development of his human nature, but at the baptism it is a question of the public declaration of his messiahship. He must be equipped with all the gifts required for his official vocation as the Christ of God.

Here is something very wonderful. A man stands before God, and does so as the Mediator and representative man, and such is his perfection that the Holy Spirit can come to him in peace and plenitude fulness. This man so loves and obeys the Father with all the heart and soul and mind that there is no sin in him to be cleansed. There is in him, of course, the very holiness of Godhead, but the point being made here is just this, that the humanity which makes him true man, is also perfectly and positively holy.

Augustine's testimony is, 'If you want to see Trinity go to Jordan.' There, one finds the Son enfleshed in human nature; the Spirit of God resting upon the Son in the form of a dove; and the Father speaking out his love and delight in the obedient Son; Father, Son, and Holy Spirit all present in the one, great manifestation of God. On this point, Bishop J.C. Ryle says something which well bears quoting: 'We may regard this as a public announcement that the work of Christ was the result of the eternal counsels of all three persons of the blessed Trinity. It was the whole Trinity which at the beginning of the creation said, "Let us make man;" it was the whole Trinity again, which at the beginning of the Gospel seemed to say, "Let us save man"' (J.C. Ryle, *Expository Thoughts on the Gospels: Matthew*, James Clarke & Co. Ltd., 1974, p.23).

The thought expressed by the godly bishop is interesting, not because it is so finely put, but because it pinpoints a highly significant feature of Christian doctrine. It brings before us something of which we hear very little today, the essentially triadic pattern that runs right through the biblical doctrine of salvation. All three persons enfolded in this simultaneous manifestation of full Godhead are present, not first of all to manifest a truth about the Divine Being and existence, but a truth about our salvation. The simple fact is that the gospel doctrines, each one in its own place, presuppose three persons in the Godhead, and that fundamental presupposition, running right through the gospel, is itself a bastion of the trinitarian teaching of Scripture.

What a testimony heaven gives to the baptized, Spirit-anointed Son. 'This is my Son, whom I love; with him I am well pleased.' This is a most significant miracle in itself. No voice came directly out of heaven before this, except at the giving of the law on Sinai. Bishop Ryle writes, 'Both occasions were of peculiar importance; it therefore seemed good to our Father in heaven to mark both with peculiar honour. At the introduction both of the Law and Gospel He Himself spoke. "God spake these words." (Exodus 20:1)' (*Expository Thoughts: Matthew*, p.23). We note in passing that on two later occasions (on the Mount of Transfiguration and in the

73

scene recorded in John 12 when Jesus was already standing in the shadow of the cross), God spoke with a voice from heaven in confirmation of the true Sonship of Jesus.

The words spoken at his baptism are not merely a reference to the special conception of Jesus as a result of the Holy Spirit's supernatural work. The reference is rather to his eternal Sonship. From all eternity he is, in an absolute and unique sense, the only begotten Son of God. This thought undergirds the love of the Father. Like the pleasure he is expressing, it is all-embracing. From eternity to eternity God loves and is well pleased with his only begotten Son. Nevertheless the reference here is in a special sense to the *man* Christ Jesus. Embraced in the divine approval are the hidden moments and years of that manhood until now, years closed off from the prying scrutiny of human curiosity, but years that were open to the all-seeing eye of the eternal God. All the patience, all the obedience, all the submission which comprised the humble, spotless walk of daily godliness — all had been seen, and now all was being attested. The Father's love of and pleasure in him were unlimited. Commentators tell us that the verbal adjective used here, *agapetos*, beloved, spells out a love that is deep-seated, thorough-going, as great as is the heart of God itself. It is also as intelligent and purposeful as is the mind of God himself.

This chapter would be incomplete without reflecting upon how gloriously the Saviour was equipped for his work. He goes from Jordan as the official, the accepted, the only anointed Saviour that the world will ever know — the only one that God has sent. Immediately all this has taken place, he is spoken of as being 'full of the Holy Spirit' (Luke 4:1). Earlier, the same writer had said that 'the child grew, and waxed strong in spirit' (2:40 A.V.) — and the implication was of a continual filling; but now he is said to be full with the plenitude fulness of the Spirit.

He goes out in another strength as well, the strength of knowing that the Father is well pleased, and loves him in the fulness of divine love. In other words, he leaves Jordan in the strength of a great, overwhelming sense of *who* he is and *what* he has come to accomplish. There can be no question now of his full acceptance of that task, or of his full messianic self-consciousness.

At Jordan his messianic Sonship was fully ratified. One more statement must be made. The ratification involved was that of a Sonship which had been sealed into spiritual union with the church — with sinful, lost men and women. It is a ratification of Jesus as baptized into us, as identified with us, with our sin and our sinnership. The great God of eternity, the representative of all the interests of the Holy Trinity does not disown his Son in this new public relationship into which he has entered. Rather, heaven acknowledges what he has pledged himself to be and to give. Heaven acknowledges him as Son although he has engaged himself to be ours. Over this entire transaction the eternal God says, 'My Son, whom I love'.

The implication of this is enormously encouraging and comforting for us as Christians. Because of the union effected in the baptism, the Head and the body — Christ and the church — are now one, even as his Sonship is being ratified by the Father. That means that the sonship of every adopted child — every son and daughter of God through grace — is being ratified also. When heaven looks down on Jordan, it looks down upon and speaks over the whole body. All who are in Christ come under the approval, the love, and the delight of the Father. Where does the Christian believer stand before God? His standing is always in Christ, and his standing goes back beyond regeneration and conversion; back beyond Calvary; back beyond Jordan; back into eternity and the love that looked upon him 'before the creation of the world' (Ephesians 1:4). We are certainly included in this Mediator-Sonship approval at Jordan.

The simple fact is that the sonship of every believer inheres in Christ. In virtue of that Sonship the Father says of every child he has, 'whom I love; with him I am well pleased'. We may not be well pleased with ourselves. If we are taught of grace we seldom can be. We have much reason to be humble. But if we have put our trust in the Lord Jesus we stand in him

— and he is perfectly righteous; and so are we, as God regards us in Christ. It was not for himself but for us that he fulfilled all righteousness. It was not for himself but for us that he was baptized with the sinner's baptism.

6
The Temptation of Jesus

'Then Jesus was led by the Spirit into the desert
to be tempted by the devil' (Matthew 4:1).

In thinking of the ministry of the Holy Spirit in the life of Jesus we have been looking at it as demonstrated in the incarnation, in his boyhood, and in the baptism of Jordan. Just as it was the Spirit who prepared a body for the eternal Son of God when the time came for him to enter this world, and who filled and empowered him beyond measure at his baptism, so the Spirit has a work to do and a role to play in the temptation as well. In fact, the very nature of our subject means that it is precisely at every main juncture of Christ's ministry that the work of the Spirit most clearly comes into view. At other times it is more hidden. The Holy Spirit seems to keep himself very much in the background, and continually to focus our attention, not upon himself, but upon Jesus.

We recall that the baptism of Jesus is an important, highly significant event from a spiritual and theological point of view. This is because one of the main elements involved in, and illustrated by, baptism is that of engrafting — of union and identity with a person or a group. In his baptism Christ was sacramentally, publicly, and officially affirming his spiritual unity with his church. As its King and Head he is completely identifying himself with all the responsibilities, obligations, and needs of every last one of his people. It is important to remember this and keep it firmly in mind because those two great events, baptism and temptation, are very closely linked together in the life of Jesus and the one sheds light upon the other.

The timing of the temptation

As we look at the temptation and explore its implications for an understanding of the Spirit's ministry to the Lord Jesus, attention must be drawn to the way Scripture introduces it and puts it into its historical, chronological context. At the very outset, it is conspicuous that it follows immediately upon the baptism of Jesus and is the very next point at which the ministry of the Spirit is explicitly reported.

All three of the Synoptic Gospels, Matthew, Mark, and Luke, record the temptation, and in each there is fascinating emphasis on *when* the temptation took place, a stress on the precise juncture in his ministry when Jesus was brought into this testing conflict. Each writer makes mention, in his own particular style, and with his own specific emphasis, of the time and the sequence in which the temptation occurred.

Matthew begins his narrative with the word 'then'. 'Then Jesus was led by the Spirit.' That refers back to what has been said at the close of the previous chapter. There we have one of the great declarations of the Father concerning his Son. It was then, as the inaugural stage of his public ministry closed on this high note, that the Spirit came and led Jesus out into the desert. This is the work of the very same Spirit who had come in the visible form of a dove and rested upon the baptized Jesus. This Spirit now takes control of the circumstances and the details of Christ's testing. He is not, of course, the agent of the temptation but it all comes under his direction and jurisdiction.

When Mark begins his account of the temptation he does so with a word that is one of the hallmarks of his writing style and that forms a particular characteristic of his Gospel. It is a word which translates as 'immediately' or 'straightway'. In this word, Mark, too, links the temptation directly with the baptism and the power of the Spirit. When he describes the action of the Spirit upon Jesus it is put even more strongly than the 'led' of Matthew. The word Mark uses is 'drive' or 'thrust'. By its use, the whole emphasis is again put upon the influence exerted upon the Saviour by the ministry of the Spirit in him. Luke also introduces and describes the temptation in a way that draws attention to its continuity with the baptism and the consequent fulness of the Spirit. 'Jesus, full of the Holy Spirit, returned from the Jordan and was led by the Spirit in the desert' (Luke 4:1).

This is the emphasis that confronts us as the Gospels open up the narrative of the temptation. It is an emphasis that drives our attention to the time sequence in which it took place and to something which otherwise might well have escaped notice. The very first thing that is required of the Lord Jesus as the baptized, declared Mediator, Saviour, and representative of his people is testing and tempting. In that baptism he was declaring himself to be the representative man, and it is highly instructive that the very first thing which is required of him as the new representative man is that he be tested.

The reason for the temptation

In the first commandment to Adam, God pointed out the fulness and the plenty with which the Lord God had endowed his environment. All around him were the fruits of the garden, all the blessings of a beneficent and bountiful Creator. That commandment put Adam into a place of probation, a place of testing. One tree — and only one — was set completely out of bounds for him. Around it and its fruit was placed the divine prohibition — 'You must not . . .' That single prohibition took man into a situation where his obedience would be brought under searching trial.

The last Adam too, is led into a place of testing; obedience is once more to be tested in human nature. The first obligation laid upon the Saviour as he publicly takes up his saving work is one which lies at the very core of man's relationship to God. It is the question of obedience or disobedience. The first thing the Father requires of the Spirit-filled Son, the first demand of heaven upon this last Adam, is identical with what was required of and laid upon the first Adam; it is obedience.

It is amazing that the very first thing God does with this Spirit-filled man is bring him into a place of probation where his obedience will be tried and tested by Satan. That is not the usual picture we have of what happens when men become filled with the Holy Spirit — but it is a biblical one, and it is a solemn, serious, and utterly realistic one.

For the first Adam the place of probation was devastating and damaging. It involved conflict and struggle. So it was for the last Adam and so it will be for every believer. Temptation is not an alien experience in the life of faith. Faith and its obedience will invariably and inevitably come under testing and trial. 'Do not be surprised', said an apostle, 'at the painful trial you are suffering' (1 Peter 4:12).

This event in the life of Jesus then, is neither strange nor alien to us. In fact, it is a part of all human and Christian experience. The biblical narrative covers old, familiar ground. The fact that the temptation follows immediately on his baptism, hard on the heels of the public assumption of his saving ministry, strongly suggests that the last Adam must enter the conflict at the very point where the first Adam had failed, and in his failure, lost all. The redemptive work and ministry of Christ is to begin precisely where man's blessing, man's walk with God, had been breached and blasted and lost by Adam. Once more conflict is to be joined between the single representative of man and the representative of evil. The ancient, world-old battle, in which all are caught up, is to be renewed in almost exactly the same form as it took at the very dawn of human history.

The conflict is to be renewed in an extremely interesting arena and in an extremely interesting manner. In essence it is the very same conflict as the first; essentially the same weapons are to be used, and the very same issues are to be at stake. It is a moral and spiritual battle, and it is to centre around the question of man's obedience. Will this Adam stand or fall? This time there is to be one great distinction — the outcome is to be entirely different. At the very place where human nature, in the first Adam, failed, human nature in the last Adam is to triumph and come through to victory.

The leading in the temptation

As soon as our Lord sets out to meet the test, it is plain that he is already on the pathway of obedience. He is being led by the Spirit. The implications of this simple statement should not go unnoticed. 'Led by the Spirit' clearly means that it is under the direction and guidance of the Spirit that the process of testing is inaugurated and that, in a very real sense, it will continue. There is no question but that this representative man will be tested to the very outer limits of human endurance. The trial will breach even all those barriers with which God always limits and restricts the testing of his children. But there will be a ministry of the Spirit, strengthening the human frame, sustaining the human soul of the Saviour. It is not possible to enter extensively, or precisely, into what that ministry includes. Even so, that the Spirit is deeply and intimately involved is beyond doubt. It is the Spirit-filled man who goes to grapple with temptation.

This is really an astounding occurrence. The Son of Man is led out into the wilderness by the Holy Spirit in order that he be brought under the tempting, testing power of the evil spirit. All this just when he had been anointed and filled with the Spirit, and just when his Sonship had been ratified and attested from heaven. Surely there is something wrong with this order; this is not the sequence we expect in Spirit-dominated lives; this is far too strange to understand.

But this sequence seems strange only because our thinking on temptation, testing, and the work of the Spirit in general is too one-sided. A rounded appreciation of the biblical teaching, and acquaintance with solid Christian experience, will reveal that this is exactly the pattern into which blessing and temptation frequently fall. It is a pattern with which believers are very familiar; first blessing, then testing. Often the case is that the greater the blessing, the more severe the testing.

This very ministry of the Spirit that we find here demonstrates one of the great norms of Christian experience. It is one characteristic of the Christian faith that not only belongs to, but actually attests, sonship. The apostle Paul teaches that leading by the Spirit is one of the marks of true sonship. 'Those who are led by the Spirit of God are sons of God' (Romans 8:14). No sooner is Jesus attested as Son than this leading feature of sonship is seen in him and manifested by him. Let it comfort the heart of every true child of God that the 'elder brother' himself was also under the leading of the Holy Spirit and his constraints and guidance in the 'days of his flesh'. The ministry of the Holy Spirit has been experienced, tested, approved by the Saviour himself. We too can readily and fully trust ourselves to his leading and guidance.

It was, no doubt, a very blessed experience for our Lord to be filled, empowered, and led by the Spirit in this way. But this ministry was not merely to comfort and encourage the Lord Jesus but to activate his own human obedience and extend its perfection into realms where it had not, thus far, been tested or exercised. It was part of that wider process by which, 'although he was a son, he learned obedience from what he suffered' (Hebrews 5:8). As he went out to the wilderness under the leading of the Spirit the Lord was taking the first public steps in his mediatorial obedience. He is not only being led, he is following, in complete submission and obedience to the Father's will as that is unveiled for him by the Spirit. It is in following that he finds and takes the pathway of obedience.

This was merely the beginning of a hard and arduous way for him — although he always delighted in it (Psalm 40:8). It was to be a way of total and absolute obedience: a way that was to end in suffering, and an obedience that was to mark every step to death. God's eternal Son goes to represent us; he goes filled and anointed by the Spirit; he goes willingly, 'obedient to death — even death on a cross!' (Philippians 2:8); above all, he goes as the *man* Christ Jesus. He stood where every Christian stands when under the power of temptation. 'He had to be made like his brothers in every way' (Hebrews 2:17).

From the way Luke speaks of the leading of the Spirit, it is clear that not only was Jesus led into the desert, or as far as the desert, but that he was under the same leading all through the forty days spent there. The Spirit was with him all through the wilderness experience; and that means all through the temptation of which the wilderness experience speaks. This helps to clarify a very common misconception about the temptation of the Lord. The fact that it is the Spirit who leads him *to* the wilderness, and *in* the wilderness indicates who ordered the temptation. Was it Satan? The answer is a very emphatic no! This testing was ordained and organized by God. Satan, of course, does the tempting, but through it all he is unaware that he is not, ultimately, in full charge of the event. That control is in God's sovereign hands and it is being exercised through the divine Spirit.

This temptation of the Lord Jesus was in the eternal purpose and will of God. He must be brought to the place of trial and he must come forth from it with a tested, proved, personal obedience. It is all part of what fits him as a perfect, sympathetic High Priest and as a faithful one as well. It is 'because he himself suffered when he was tempted, he is able to help those who are being tempted' (Hebrews 2:18). This was not of Satan's doing. Rather, because of 'God's set purpose and foreknowledge' (Acts 2:23), it was necessary for Satan to be there.

The setting of the temptation

Everyone knows that it was to the 'wilderness' that Jesus was led by the Spirit. Few stop to think about the place, or the significance of it to the entire testing. Why should the temptation take place in the wilderness?

We might think that the wilderness was a very strange setting for the temptation of the last Adam. On consideration a comparison may be drawn. The comparison leads to contrast, a very stark, very powerful contrast. It is the contrast between a garden and a wilderness; between the circumstances of the first temptation and this one. The first Adam was tested and tried under ideal conditions; surrounded by beauty and harmony and plenty. But the circumstances under which the last Adam is tempted are totally different. Desert conditions, no growth, no trees, no fruit, no food. Why the change? Why the stark, almost repulsive, contrast? Why is the last Adam to be tried under such utterly uncongenial circumstances?

To answer that question we pose another. What turns a garden into a wilderness? It is neglect that accounts for the change. Lack of care is responsible for the weeds and rubbish. The Bible teaches (Genesis 3) that the one thing that changes the garden into a wilderness is the curse of almighty God upon man's sin. 'To Adam he said . . . cursed is the ground because of you . . . It will produce thorns and thistles for you' (Genesis 3:17,18).

In his infinite mercy and goodness God has not brought the worst features of the curse upon every area of the earth. By dint of hard work, men get growth and fruitage from the soil. Yet, large tracts of the earth's surface are barren and inhospitable and desolate; man is unable to survive in them. By its wilderness places the earth reminds us that we live under the curse. It is to the very place that epitomizes sin and its effects that Christ comes to free the creation from that curse.

What a difference there is in the testing of Adam and Christ. Adam is tested in an environment filled, not with the curse of God, but his blessing. Christ must begin his task under the actual conditions which Adam's failure has brought about. He must begin among the wreckage and the ruin and the chaos that sin has wrought in the creation of God. At the outset of his public work he is brought into the wilderness, in a physical as well as a spiritual sense. His surroundings must drive home to his mind and heart the sheer enormity of his task. The wilderness in which the temptation is set must reflect, for him, the spiritual state of those he has come to redeem and save and bring home out of the wilderness to the Father's house.

Men's hearts may no longer be described as a garden. It is the wilderness that now most accurately reflects the heart and the soul and the mind of man as he is by nature. The curse and blight of sin are written as deeply into our nature as they are written into the nature of the world in which we live. When Christ, the Son of God, comes to implement our redemption he must begin with us where we are by nature. He must begin in the place where sin has taken us and left us. Where has sin taken us? Where has sin left us? It has left us in the place of God's curse. The wildernesses and deserts of this world are desolate and barren places. But desolate as they may be, they are only a pale reflection of the desolation and barrenness of the soul without Christ and still under the curse of God.

The very setting of the temptation gives us an insight into the nature of the redemptive requirement underlying Christ's mission. The last Adam is tempted in a situation that forced one great fact in upon him — the glaring evidence of failure in the first Adam. In its own way the wilderness reinforced the devil's message and helped sharpen the barbs of his attack. He was operating amidst the actual evidence of former conquest, with tokens of his power to blight and blast the work of God on every side. *The first man couldn't stand, and if he couldn't stand against me, why should you?*

The testing in the temptation

What was the actual test Jesus faced? The testing actually begins with a query concerning his Sonship. 'If you are the Son of God.' At the baptism in Jordan heaven had opened for Jesus: the Spirit had come down upon him: the Father had spoken. The attestation and approval had been clear — 'my Son, whom I love'. Now comes the evil one and says, 'If you are the Son of God . . .' The question is an old, familiar one. The accents also sound familiar. 'Did God really say . . .?' It is the same old devil, with the same old story, sowing the same old seed. It is the seed which flourished so well in the soil of Eden. It is the seed of doubt in the truthfulness of God.

The satanic tactics have not really changed. They never do. But there is a barb here that may not be evident at first sight. It is as though the devil was taunting our Lord. 'You — you who have gone and joined yourself in baptismal and spiritual union with a sinful, fallen, people — you, the Son of God? What nonsense! God will not have you now, you've stained and spoiled your Sonship.' In other words, it was the baptiz-

85

ed, mediatorial Sonship that was being spoken about. The eternal Sonship was — and must ever be — beyond the reach of Satan's power. But had the man Christ Jesus, the incarnate Son, not left himself vulnerable? Satan thought he had found a chink in the armour and he attacked it.

Every Christian is involved in this transaction. In the baptism of Christ there was attestation of all the sons with whom he was one in his baptism. Here in the temptation there is a counterpart to that. Here the corporate body, the sons who are one with him, shares in the attack made upon him. The scene is re-enacted in Christian experience and every believer has felt the force and power of temptation. But the victory of the past, in Christ, carries over to the present conflict; no true child has ever been lost; 'They shall never perish' (John 10:28). There is no need to elaborate on the temptations; they all proceed on the same principle. 'You, the Son of God — and hungry! You, the Son of God — and you have so little of this world, or its goods!' The temptations of all the children, in every age, are echoes of this sour dirge.

Another element in the testing is this; it is all aimed at trying to make Jesus forsake the stance he has just taken up so openly; that of representative man. Now Satan tempts him to leave that ground by the exercise of his own divine nature. 'If you are the Son of God make these stones bread'; in other words, 'Use your divine nature to sustain and save your human nature.' Had Jesus done that he would have been forsaking his place as true representative man. He would have been using ways and means which are not open to any of his brothers, and in so doing he would no longer be 'like' them. More, he would have been denying one of the cardinal principles involved in his incarnation — the dependence inherent in creaturehood and true manhood. In turning aside the temptation, he honours and ratifies that principle. He says, 'Man does not live on bread alone.' One word in that utterance conveys immense solace to the heart of every believer. He said *Man*. The application to himself of that word from Moses meant that the Lord refused to abandon what incarnation involved, that circumscribed circle of dependent manhood.

The significance of what Jesus said is this. Man needs — and can have — more than this world or its bread alone can ever give to him. To make much of this world and its bread is natural to us. Thus we fail to do justice to our highest interests as men — to acknowledge what our humanity actually involves. We put bread before the Word and worship of God and so deny our spiritual being by emphasizing only bodily needs. We thank God that there was one man, who was truly man, who refused to become something other than what God intended man to be. Jesus' life and work ensure that men *need* not live by bread alone. Throughout his conflict, Jesus demonstrates how to set one's goals and perspectives by the Word of God and how to use it to live. That is what we consider next.

The defence in the temptation

That Jesus should lay hold of Scripture and use it to overcome Satan is not surprising — at least, not if we know anything about the help and the power of God's holy Word in our own experience. Jesus was there trying out, proving, and approving the weapons which alone are to be the weapons of the warfare of his people. We have much to learn from this, particularly in our use of the Bible and its truth in our inward conflicts. It is 'the sword of the Spirit' (Ephesians 6:17); and we must learn to wield it to good purpose in our own spiritual warfare. The Saviour himself, with his constantly reiterated refrain, 'it is written', epitomizes the truth asserted so strongly by the apostle, 'The weapons we fight with are not the weapons of the world. On the contrary, they have divine power to demolish strongholds' (2 Corinthians 10:4). One of the great dangers for the individual believer — as for the corporate church — is that of trusting to means and methods which achieve success for the world. The Bible warns against such an attitude. It always lays stress on spiritual factors — faith, prayer, obedience, the Scriptures, the Holy Spirit; and every one of those factors, used trustingly, points us back to, and links us with, the Lord Jesus himself.

An aspect of Christ's mediatorial work which tends to fall

out of sight today is strongly stressed by John, the apostle of love. It is John who says, 'The reason the Son of God appeared was to destroy the devil's work' (1 John 3:8). The word translated 'destroy' is very interesting. It means to 'break up' or to 'loosen' and was used, for example, of 'casting off' the ropes securing a ship to a pier. So, Jesus was commissioned to 'loosen', 'cast off', 'break up', take the 'coherence' out of the devil's operations. Viewed in the light of that purpose, what a triumph his victory in the wilderness proves to have been. It was the precursor of other, greater triumphs for the Lord, and was achieved with weapons still freely available to every Christian.

What must be observed are the scriptures that he does use. They are texts that could be used by the very humblest of his followers in every age. In this connection it is encouraging that he does not do what he could most readily have done — go to any of the great messianic texts and scriptures which belong so particularly and peculiarly to himself. Jesus goes only to words that any of the sons and daughters can go to at any time. He will avail himself of no help, no weapon, no strategy, that is not fully and freely available to the very least of his brethren.

It is significant that the scriptures he does quote and use are all taken from one specific book in the Bible, Deuteronomy. When and where did those words come from the mouth of God? They came to the church when she was in the wilderness, journeying on through all kinds of difficulties, towards the land of God's promise. Here is the great Head of the church, and he, too, is in the midst of a wilderness experience. It is most ironical that Jesus should have gone to the Pentateuch for the words which, as he says, proceed from the mouth of God; and particularly so that he should have gone to Deuteronomy. It is ironical for the simple reason that no section of the entire Bible has suffered so badly from unbelieving, critical scholarship over the last hundred years or so, as the first five books and, in particular, Deuteronomy. In fact, the book that Jesus so clearly attested as being the Word of God is still being used by God's people in the midst of the wilderness, and will be until the last believer arrives home and there is no more need of the 'wilderness' book.

It is certain that the Lord often used the Scriptures to help and sustain his own heart. It is marvellous but not really surprising that it should be so. He is true man, and what he prescribes for other men he will practise himself. He used them for practical reasons for himself also. His human mind was enlightened by the Spirit-given Word and his heart fortified. Clearly, he loved and knew those Scriptures perfectly and used them at other times and for other purposes than at the temptation. It is pleasant to think of this in our Saviour. In the wilderness, no doubt one place from which he would have comforted his heart would have been Psalm 46:

> *God is our refuge and our strength,*
> *in straits a present aid;*
> *Therefore, although the earth remove,*
> *we will not be afraid.*
> (Scottish Psalter)

This was one of the scriptures to which the great Martin Luther often resorted when things seemed to be going against him. 'Come Philip,' he would say to his colleague, Melancthon, 'Let us encourage ourselves in God; let us sing in Psalm 46.' It should be a marvellous encouragement to the believer when tried and tested, that our Lord himself knew what it was to stand in a place where he had to look up and where, in his own experience, he knew deliverance and help from the Father, by the Spirit, through the Word.

As well as the Word, Jesus uses the weapon of faith, described elsewhere in the Bible as the 'shield' of the Christian armour (Ephesians 6:16). The fact that the Lord Jesus exercised faith is, perhaps, not one about which we often hear. But here, too, he is like his brethren. One of the great messianic Psalms that takes us into the painful intimacies and extremities of his great agony on the cross, predicted this very faith of him. 'He trusted on the LORD', it said. It went on to specify that trust and the kind of situation in which he would exercise it. 'He trusted on the LORD that he would deliver

89

him' (Psalm 22:8 A.V.). That embraces, not only the suffering of Calvary (where it was actually thrown at him as a taunt), but this wilderness temptation as well. It was to God that he looked for deliverance, and to God through his Word. That Jesus put his confidence and trust in that Word should undergird our confidence in it also. Where he trusted, we may safely follow; where his feet have been held, he himself will keep us safely too.

We must not forget that he had the indwelling Holy Spirit as a weapon, as well. The Spirit was leading, guiding, sustaining, and upholding the Son of Man in this great hour of need and testing. The Christian believer has the same Spirit indwelling him also. Although this may not be in the measureless way that the Saviour had this indwelling, the Spirit is in every believer in greater or lesser degree. It is the believer's responsibility to be 'filled' with the Spirit and to 'walk' in the Spirit.

The achievement of the temptation

The fruits of victory, we are told, have been sweet to the heroes and conquerors of history. The fruits of spiritual conquest certainly are. Wherever and whenever a believer experiences and enjoys such victory it always relates back to Christ. It is in him, and in him alone, that 'we are more than conquerors'. Our representative fulfilled all righteousness for us. He goes to the place of testing and remains in it, self-consciously and deliberately, as *man*. As our representative he demonstrates not what absolute Godhead can achieve, not what omniscience or omnipotence can achieve — even when found in human nature. He is demonstrating what the Word of God and the Spirit of God can achieve for man. On this we must insist. His is mediatorial obedience; therefore it has to be obedience rendered in the nature of those he came to redeem. It was the obedience of a man; God's man, yes, but our man too.

The temptation emphasizes another feature already noted about Christ's identification with us — that it was marked by one great exception. That exception was manifested and perfected in just such personal experience as in this wilderness temptation. It also makes the temptation and its triumphant achievement precious to our faith. Paradoxically that one exception is what draws and binds us to him with great power and comfort. He 'has been tempted in every way, just as we are — yet was without sin' (Hebrews 4:15). To such a Saviour we may all turn with perfect confidence. In him we will certainly 'receive mercy and find grace to help us in our time of need' (Hebrews 4:16).

The ministry of the Spirit in this climactic event in the life and work of Christ was of paramount importance. Many aspects of it are veiled from our view and we dare probe it only as far as Scripture itself allows. Perhaps the most explicit, and in many ways the most encouraging message it has for the Christian believer is simply that it underwrites very powerfully the true humanity of Christ. It proves that, as the great representative of his people, his identification with them and their circumstances has been perfect and complete.

7
The Public Ministry of Jesus

*'Jesus returned to Galilee in the power of the
Spirit, and news about him spread through the whole
countryside'* (Luke 4:14).

Those words of Luke take up the theme of the Spirit's work in
the life and ministry of Christ at its next point of emergence,
and provide us with a direct link to the previous chapter, the
ministry of the Spirit in the temptation. It is the 'peak' events
in the Lord's life which afford us glimpses of the Spirit's
ministry in him and to him. Although the Spirit, as the in-
spirer of Scripture, has largely veiled his own operations,
those glimpses reveal that he had a very real and important
ministry in the incarnate Son.

Although Luke here links the powerful ministry of Jesus
immediately and directly to the return from the wilderness, he
does not say that the events he proceeds to describe constitute
Jesus' first public appearance after his baptism and temptation in the wilderness. This is an important fact for us to
keep in mind and it is one which Luke himself makes clear
from several details he gives in the passage following our text.
The narrative shows that vivid accounts of his ministry had
preceded this visit of Jesus to Nazareth. For example, the
words of Jesus recorded in verse 23 indicate that people
already knew about many of the great healing miracles: 'Surely you will quote this proverb to me: "Physician, heal
yourself! Do here in your home town what we have heard that
you do in Capernaum."'

Luke's statement is significant apart from the events he
goes on to relate in the verses following. What it does is give a

broad overview of the stirring months which had been making the ministry of Jesus a talking-point far and wide, news of which had reached even Nazareth. What Luke passes over is touched on by Matthew and Mark and, in a fascinating and supplementary way, by John (John 1:19-4:42). It is this powerful, preceding ministry which Luke has in mind as he introduces the events he wishes to record about this visit to the home town of Nazareth.

The blessings of a tested obedience

That prior ministry radiating out from Capernaum, and known amongst commentators as the Great Galilean Ministry, is directly associated with the crisis events which have been occupying us already. But what Luke says here about the return of Jesus into Galilee shows how the Lord Jesus fulfilled his entire ministry, and illustrates one of the main principles of the incarnation. If we fail to grasp this, then we may well fail to appreciate how fully, as man, he drew his power not directly from his own divine nature but from the executor of Godhead, the Holy Spirit. We may fail to see, as well, how truly and fully he was identified with his 'brothers' in their humanity. As the creeds and confessions have it, he was 'very man'.

Luke's words here must not be misunderstood. He is emphasizing very strongly that the whole ministry of Jesus, in all its aspects and all its scope, takes its rise from the victory in which he returned out of the wilderness temptation; and specifically from the power which now rested so fully upon him; 'Jesus returned to Galilee in the power of the Spirit'. The reports of his amazing work, and his teaching and preaching, are to be understood as consequences of two critical factors. They trace back, firstly, to the anointing at Jordan, flowing out of the measureless fulness of the Spirit with which that commissioning unction endowed him; and secondly, to the obedience that he brought back out of the wilderness, giving him a newly-won prerogative — the messianic entitlement to the use of that power with which the Spirit's plenitude had anointed him.

That thought of a tested obedience requires emphasis. There is an element in it which explains one aspect of the telling authority which rested on the public ministry of Jesus. But that element also illustrates a vital truth about the Spirit-filled life of the believer. As Jesus returned to Galilee in the power of the Spirit, he returned also in the power of an obedience which had been actualized and proved with every step which took him triumphantly through the fires of affliction and temptation to tested perfection.

A very simple illustration may help. Climbers, coastguards, lifeboat men — people whose very lives depend upon such matters — use ropes that have a proven breaking strain. The process by which that breaking strain was assessed meant that the ropes concerned were actually tested right up to the specified limits — far beyond any strain they would be required to bear in actual use. They have a tested perfection. Out over a cliff the climbers know that that rope will do all that is ever asked of it. So, the perfection of Christ's mediatorial obedience is a proven, tested perfection — not just a theoretical obedience. Mediatorial obedience made the man Christ Jesus spiritually and self-consciously strong for his saving work on the cross — 'The prince of this world is coming. He has no hold on me', he said; and again, in relation to the will of the Father (the ultimate test of all obedience), 'I always do what pleases him' (John 14:30; 8:29).

The implications of this are very interesting and very important for the Christian life. This Spirit-filled Son is also the obedient Son. Obedience, with the conscience void of offence toward God and toward men which belongs only to obedience, is one of the fortified strongholds of the godly life. Indeed, it is the surest hallmark of the Spirit's regenerating and sanctifying work in the heart of man. Obedience and the indwelling fulness of the Spirit are correlates of the godly life; they always go together. The entire New Testament witness teaches us that obedience is the most characteristic mark of the Spirit's saving work in man. It is the very stuff of holiness and true godliness. People who are truly filled with the Spirit will demonstrate it, along the same avenues as the Master himself — they will be holy men and women; people who love the commandments of God and who strive, by his grace, to keep them inviolate.

One cannot help but wonder sometimes, if his own temptations were not very strongly before the mind of the risen Saviour when he said to the church at Ephesus: 'To him who overcomes I will give the right to eat from the tree of life, which is in the paradise of God' (Revelation 2:7). Because he overcame in the wilderness he knows what conflict is like, and his perfect work enables and entitles him to open the paradise of God to his own. The two things, his victory and ours, are linked in another of those marvellous, majestic statements of the risen Christ: 'To him who overcomes, I will give the right to sit with me on my throne, just as I overcame and sat down with my Father on his throne' (Revelation 3:21).

The kingly authority of his ministry

In dealing with Jesus' ministry after the inaugural events of baptism and temptation, Matthew mentions, very briefly, the imprisonment of John the Baptist. He then details, briefly too, but very significantly, the calling of some of the disciples by Jesus (Matthew 4:18-22). In this way Matthew gives content to Luke's statement that 'Jesus returned . . . in the power of the Spirit'. In fact, we have an exposition from Matthew of those things which Luke only implies, the things which made Jesus 'famous'. It begins with his calling of the disciples. The significance of the calling of the disciples to the subject of the Spirit's powerful ministry in our Lord should not be ignored.

This action of the triumphant, obedient Jesus is basic and fundamental to an overall biblical interpretation of his work. This is the Messiah King of Old Testament prediction. One of the many of those predictive prophecies states, 'Gird your sword upon your side, O mighty one; clothe yourself with splendour and majesty. In your majesty ride forth victoriously in behalf of truth, humility and righteousness . . . Let your sharp arrows pierce the hearts of the king's enemies; let the nations fall beneath your feet. Your throne, O God, will last for ever and ever' (Psalm 45:3-6). That, partly, belongs to the second coming of Christ in his glorious power, but it has reference also to his first coming and to the kind of kingly triumph which we have in this very part of his ministry.

Coming fresh from the scenes of temptation with a victory which bestowed all the rights of conquest, with an absolute plenitude of the Spirit, and in the authority of that Spirit's power, the Lord Jesus began to call disciples to himself. He did this partly to have around him and with him trophies of his victory, but also to teach those men, and fit them to be leaders and overseers of the church — the kingdom which he was going to build on the very site, and over the very ruins, of Satan's empire. Against this church the 'gates' (the combined wisdom) of hell should not prevail. Their preaching was to win others, and every new convert was a new trophy, wrested from the adversary by the Holy Spirit, on the ground of the perfect obedience displayed and operative at the very point where the battle was lost by the first man. Calvary was still to come, but these were the first obedient steps of God's kingly Mediator.

The power of his prophetic ministry

It is those very men, called to Jesus, taught by him to preach, themselves renewed, anointed, and empowered by the Holy Spirit, who are to go out as his heralds and envoys to proclaim salvation through faith in his name. His own powerful preaching ministry went before them. It was one of the methods of their training — listening to the master preacher of the ages. In looking at this aspect of the Lord's ministry we are again confronted with some of the things which Luke meant when he said that 'Jesus returned to Galilee in the power of the Spirit'. It is a further exposition of what that power was, and what the Lord Jesus did with it. Faced with his magnetic preaching power, his authority, and his initial popularity, we are being given a still more detailed picture of what the Saviour did when confirmed into his public ministry by the Holy Spirit

Matthew says that Jesus went all through Galilee, 'teaching in their synagogues, preaching the good news of the kingdom, and healing every disease and sickness among the people' (Matthew 4:23). That is a very informative description of the ministry of our Lord. One thing comes out very strikingly from Matthew's words, as it does from Luke's, and that is the place which preaching occupies in that ministry. It lies so powerfully in the forefront of all that Jesus did that men ever since have spoken — and rightly so — of the primacy of preaching in his work. This is the exercise of what theology speaks of as the prophetic office of Christ. For this, he was powerfully and specially equipped by the Holy Spirit of God.

Matthew's description of the actual work of the Lord Jesus is significant: '*teaching* in their synagogues, *preaching* the good news of the kingdom'. It is important to notice that between preaching and teaching there is, biblically, a distinct difference, though they are very closely allied — so much so, that good preaching includes and encompasses teaching. The biblical emphasis, nevertheless, is not the same for both. The word used in the New Testament for preaching means heralding, announcing, proclaiming. Teaching, on the other hand, indicates the careful imparting of more detailed information regarding the announcement that was made. And while Jesus taught in that sense, the emphasis here lies upon his preaching — his proclamation of the good news of the kingdom.

In his preaching Jesus spoke of the work of salvation as the kingdom or reign of heaven. He did so, of course, in order to indicate the supernatural character, origin, and purpose of our salvation. Salvation traces back to the grace of the God of heaven and so should magnify his glory. And by his use of the term 'kingdom' the Lord Jesus safeguarded that truth so precious to all believers, that everything — not least the salvation of sinners through his sacrifice — is subservient to God's glory.

The spotlight of the Spirit

One of the main ministries of the Holy Spirit, according to New Testament teaching, is that he focuses attention all the time on Jesus Christ and his work for our salvation. A sure sign of Spirit-filled, Spirit-directed, Spirit-anointed preaching is that it spotlights Jesus and exalts him as 'The only Redeemer of God's elect'. Although we might at first blush think it strange that it should be so, this primary characteristic of the Spirit's presence and power is strongly manifested in Jesus' own preaching.

When men have studied his preaching and his message, what has often struck them is the unabashed candour with which Jesus points men so exclusively to himself. Without embarrassment, he presents himself as the answer to the very deepest needs of the human heart and invites them to trust in himself. He promises, in the strongest possible terms, that all who come to him will find spiritual peace and rest and lose their burdens. He claims that no single person can come to the Father but through him. In anyone else but Jesus those claims would sound grandiose, ridiculous — grotesque even — but coming from him they carry a weight, a responsibility, a ring of factual truth which have impressed men powerfully ever since. What in others we would condemn as blasphemous, in him we hail as divine. Such pronouncements as he made are uttered in the power and under the anointing of the Holy Spirit.

Rightly understood, all this should not offend. It must be considered within the context of the other, larger, claim he made, and with which this class of statement is perfectly consonant — his claim, made again and again, to be God. Indeed, this very aspect of his ministry is just what should be expected to accompany such uncluttered claims to unique, divine Sonship and it should encourage us to trust the Saviour.

There is nothing surprising in this element in Christ's ministry. In empowering Christ to preach, the Spirit ministers according to the strictest principle of all his work in, through, and for the Son: 'He will bring glory to me by taking from what is mine and making it known to you' (John 16:14). That leading characteristic, that ultimate proof of what Spirit is at work in a man's ministry, is seen at its highest and clearest in the ministry of Christ himself. It was eminently fitting that it should be so. Indeed, it could not have been otherwise. Here, too, Christ abides by the principle of his incarnation; in the realm of his prophetic, preaching ministry, as in the others, he draws all the power from Godhead, not directly through his own divine nature, but through the plenitude of the Spirit. The Spirit honours the Son and Mediator. It is the mark of his ministry.

The thrust of his message

Christ's preaching is part of what lay behind his reputation through the regions of Judea. It was a fruit of his anointing and obedience. His words came with freshness, power, and authority. Men had never heard this kind of preaching, or this kind of message before. Just as this was true for the Master, so it has often been true for his disciples. It has been Spirit-filled men and Spirit-filled preaching that have advanced the gospel in every age. That is not to say that a Spirit-filled ministry will necessarily be popular; the crowds did not like some of the things that the Lord Jesus had to say to them, and so there were periods when many went back from him. Nonetheless, the overall impression given in the New Testament is of multitudes crowding around his ministry.

There was one note in the Saviour's preaching which merits attention. It is a characteristic of gospel preaching — so much so, that where it is not present then the gospel is not present either. That single, vital note is the need for men to repent, to turn away from sin to God, and to do that through putting their trust in Christ. He made those elements of his message the very prerequisites of salvation. Without repentance and trust in him men could not be saved.

This message relates, of course, in a very basic and essential way, to the message which John the Baptist had proclaimed about Jesus immediately on his return from the temptation. That was a proclamation of personal suffering and sacrifice defined in terms of Old Testament teaching and delivered to a people who were steeped in Old Testament thought. 'Look, the Lamb of God, who takes away the sin of the world!' (John 1:29). All the implications of this doctrine were readily accepted by the Saviour, and although he deliberately refrained from spelling out to his disciples the death of the cross until the last six months of his ministry, it undergirded everything he did and said from the very beginning. His claims, invitations, and promises all looked onwards to the climactic achievement of his death. It was on that basis that the doctrine of repentance was central to his message of salvation.

The constituency to which his ministry came

It seems that this is what Luke wishes to stress. The very way he begins his account of Jesus' ministry with the visit to Nazareth meshes with the wider framework of his Gospel. He specially treats of Jesus come to bring salvation not only to the Jews but to Gentiles — to all who should believe on him. It is most appropriate that he should begin with the story of Jesus' preaching and his rejection in Nazareth. All this unveils Jesus as the anointed Redeemer who does not consider himself tied down to bringing the glad tidings to Jews only. His gospel is for men as men — indeed, for men as sinners.

What Jesus does in the synagogue at Nazareth highlights our theme very powerfully. He stood up as a sign of his wish to officiate for the remaining part of the service on that Sabbath; this was customary for visiting rabbis or teachers. Of course, by this time people were very curious to hear Jesus. All of them had heard about his preaching power and here he is, for the first time, in his local congregation. Jesus then read from Isaiah 61:1,2 along with a single phrase from Isaiah 58:6. What he read to those particular people illumines, illustrates, and confirms the ministry of the Holy Spirit in his work. 'The Spirit of the Lord is on me, because he has anointed me to preach good news to the poor. He has sent me to proclaim freedom for the prisoners and recovery of sight for the blind, to release the oppressed, to proclaim the year of the Lord's favour.'

Jesus then did what he was continually doing all through his ministry. He related that ministry to the prophetic word of Old Testament Scripture; rooting his right, and authority, and power, and claims, — back into the things God had already revealed about Messiah. There is absolutely no question that it was within this framework that the Lord Jesus understood and interpreted his own ministry.

Here the claim is very specific. It is the claim to be standing in the place of the Anointed One. He is claiming to have been endued with the unction, the power, the authority of the Spirit which would identify Messiah. More, he is claiming that his works are all accomplished in the Spirit's power and that their very character confirms him as Messiah. The power and authority of his works, and the people on whom they are done all fit into the ministry foretold of Messiah. The poor, the prisoner, the blind, the bruised — those are the people who come under the power of his Spirit-filled ministry. It is all an indicator of the arrival of God's time of grace and favour.

What a deep realization Jesus had of the needs of men. An imperfect appreciation of man's spiritual state inevitably results in an inadequate remedy. But Jesus is realistic in his analysis and his descriptions. It is a characteristic of his preaching that he always referred in a very plain way to the enormous spiritual needs of men. He saw, and felt, and so he preached about, and to, the brokenness and the sinfulness of men.

As he preached like this, in the power of the Spirit, he honoured the Word of God. It was at the very heart of his preaching. His diagnosis of men's condition was founded upon it. This is another infallible mark of a Spirit-filled ministry — it will honour the Word of God, and it will major, not on what man says, but on what God has revealed.

The doctrine he preached (from the Word of God) and the manner in which he preached it (by the Spirit of God) demonstrated, and do still, the anointing which he claimed, and to which the prophecy referred. His own people there in Nazareth were made to wonder 'at the gracious words that came from his lips' as he ministered to man's need through the Spirit who anoints. May that sense of wonder long prevail.

101

8
The Works of Jesus

'But if I drive out demons by the Spirit of God,
then the kingdom of God has come upon you'
(Matthew 12:28).

One of the most interesting aspects of the life and work of the Lord Jesus is his performance of works of unusual power, the miracles. These quickly attracted a very large and highly enthusiastic following to his wonderful, but brief, public ministry. The picture conveyed by the Gospels is of rapidly-growing excitement and ever-increasing crowds. From the beginning there were people thronging him wherever he went. Even when he withdrew from the cities and towns into the deserts the crowds followed and were so huge that it was almost impossible for him to get any peace or rest.

It was this stirring interest in the new prophetic ministry, and particularly in the healing miracles, that intensified the crowds and aroused, first the attention, then the bitter opposition of the scribes and Pharisees against him. This is the setting of the text, and it is because these leaders of Israel were accusing him of doing his miracles by the power of Satan that we get this further glimpse into the theme of the Spirit's ministry and power in Jesus.

Significantly this is one of the Lord's own statements of the theme and is actually the first we have taken into account. Clearly, he is aware of the importance of the Holy Spirit in his work. He is conscious of his messiahship and the fulness of his anointing and the power that this involves and bestows. The statement of the text and the setting in which it comes are, like the baptism of Jordan, rich in trinitarian overtones.

That emphasis is reinforced by the forthright declaration of Jesus that attributing his works of power to Satan rather than the Holy Spirit constitutes the worst blasphemy. It provides, even if almost incidentally, a powerful defence not only of his own work but of the Spirit's personality, deity, and power. His words are words of serious and solemn reaction to a wickedly sinful suggestion and, as such, they should be carefully noted.

The source of miraculous power

This assertion of Jesus that he cast out demons by the power of the Spirit was made in the face of a blasphemous accusation. A demon-possessed man, blind and dumb, had been restored and healed and the crowds were so astonished that they immediately began to wonder if this really was the promised Messiah for whom Israel was waiting. That he is an unknown, humble man from Galilee leaves a note of uncertainty in their minds: 'Surely this cannot be the Son of David?' (v.23, author's translation). It is now generally agreed that by the time Jesus lived this title was a common messianic description. It is the suggestion that Jesus is the promised Messiah which, in fact, stirs up the wrath of the Pharisees against Jesus and makes them ascribe his miracles to the power of the pit. 'It is only by Beelzebub the prince of demons, that this fellow drives out demons' (v.24).

Jesus reacted swiftly and stringently against this suggestion of devilish and demonic influence in his works of power. The rigour and the strength of what he said indicate how important and how precious the ministry of the Spirit was in his own eyes. His response also confirms the importance of his own anointing and of the ministry of the Spirit in his work on earth.

The solemn warning about blasphemy against the Holy Spirit occurs in one form or another in all three of the Synoptic Gospels. A similar statement is found earlier in Luke: 'But if I drive out demons by the finger of God, then the kingdom of God has come to you' (Luke 11:20). The proof that the kingdom has now come in our Lord's own presence and ministry is that the kingdom of Satan is being robbed of its power. 'Or again, how can anyone enter a strong man's house and carry off his possessions unless he first ties up the strong man? Then he can rob his house' (v.29). The incarnate Son, anointed beyond measure with the Holy Spirit, has complete and authoritative control over the kingdom of darkness. By word and deed he is depriving Satan of those who have been in the grip of his power.

This being the case, it is little wonder that Jesus explicitly defines the claim of the Pharisees as sinfully reckless. He is not implying that Satan cannot work miracles of power. What he is saying is that Satan will never work against himself. Beelzebub does not rob his own house. The suggestion that the miracles are due to his power when they are actually freeing people from his dominion is ridiculous and absurd. We should be extremely careful about the source of anything which is claimed as a divine miracle. The source of miraculous power is to be known not by the wonder of its achievement but by its ultimate moral effects.

This very strong reaction of the Lord Jesus to those charges seems to centre not so much in concern about wrong ideas concerning himself or his works but in the dishonour being done to the Holy Spirit. That demanded, and received, one of the most solemn warnings ever to come from the lips of Jesus. It was then that he spoke of a sin for which there is no forgiveness. The light that this sheds on our theme requires that closer attention be given to this serious admonition. Firstly, however, we must consider the sort of Spirit-empowered works which called forth such bitter opposition and the Lord's solemn warning. One thing to keep in mind in regard to his warning about a sin which could not be forgiven is simply this: in the teaching of Jesus and the apostles, forgiveness and true repentance went hand in hand. They were inseparable.

Miraculous works of power
What is the definition of a New Testament miracle? A miracle has been defined as a work wrought by a divine power for a

divine purpose by means beyond the reach of mere men. That is not a complete definition for, while it does distinguish between operations of the divine and the human, it fails to distinguish between what we call the natural and the supernatural. Although the achievements of man are astounding there are many things in the 'natural' realm which he can neither understand nor manipulate.

We live in a world permeated with the 'wonderful works' of God. It has been said that the seed that multiplies in the furrow is as marvellous as the bread that multiplied in Christ's hands, and there is a sense in which that is absolutely true. We should realize that the miracle is not a greater manifestation of God's power than the recurring processes of the world around us but that it is, rather, a different manifestation of that same power. Miracle involves activities and powers of God other than those to which we have become accustomed.

Scripture indicates an unceasing activity of God in his world, but unless that activity happens to take an unusual or unexpected form, men are satisfied to think of it in terms of what they call natural laws. In this way they shut God out of his creation and enclose themselves in a completely mechanistic universe. The biblical view cuts right across this, however, and indicates that from one point of view miracle is merely the power and activity of God manifested in an unusual or unexpected manner.It is not even perfectly described by the words supernatural or supra-natural because even they tend to evade the direct implication, the presence and activity of a wise and personal God.

It is noticeable that the Bible itself never sets out to define or explain miracles from the standpoint of nature or science. Yet it never permits us to evade the divine element by putting some undefined power such as nature into the place and role of the living God. All too often, men speak as if nature were some kind of omnipotent, intelligent, and purposeful power at work everywhere in the world. This is really quite indefensible and is, at best, a poor substitute for the God revealed in Jesus Christ. The Bible highlights the moral source, the moral power, the moral aim, and particularly the moral effects which miracles had among men. The biblical concept of miracle is that of some extraordinary work of Deity transcending the ordinary laws of life and confirming the aims of special revelation.

The effect of the miracles

With his graphically descriptive style, Mark is the writer who emphasizes how quickly this ministry attracted attention from all quarters. The way the crowds flocked to Jesus in the early days of his public ministry is one of the leading themes in the first three chapters of his short Gospel. The immediate impact Jesus made on the scene of his day is conveyed in one of those quick little summaries which Mark gives every now and then: 'News about him spread quickly over the whole region of Galilee' (Mark 1:28). He makes it clear, too, that this popular interest soon spread far beyond the bounds of Galilee. 'Jesus withdrew with his disciples to the lake, and a large crowd from Galilee followed. When they heard all he was doing, many people came to him from Judea, Jerusalem, Idumea, and the regions across the Jordan and around Tyre and Sidon. Because of the crowd he told his disciples to have a small boat ready for him, to keep the people from crowding him' (Mark 3:7-9).

The influence behind this growing attention and increasing public agitation was not merely the proclamation that the kingdom of God was at hand, but the manifestation of its actual presence in the huge number of healing miracles which were performed. Men could neither close their eyes to the wonder of what was happening, nor conceal their interest and their fascination with what was going on around them. It is likely that most of us underestimate the far-reaching effects of this aspect of the Lord's ministry on the contemporary scene. No less a theologian than the sober-minded B.B. Warfield has said this: 'Disease and death must have been almost eliminated for a brief season from Capernaum and the region which lay immediately around Capernaum as a centre. No wonder the public mind was thrown into a state of profound perturbation, and, the enthusiasm spreading, men flocked from every quarter to see this great thing, questioning with one another what it all meant' (*Works*, vol. 3, p.175).

The miracles of Jesus were mostly an exercise of loving compassion towards very needy people. However, it does not do justice either to their nature or their purpose to regard them merely as a display of personal sympathy or personal concern on the part of the Saviour. There is more to them than that. From the words of the text, as well as from a number of similar references which he made, it is clear that these miracles were all performed by the power of the Holy Spirit. The Lord Jesus did not perform his powerful works by drawing on the resources of his own divine nature, but by working in and through the power of the Holy Spirit. In other words, in this fascinating and important area of his earthly ministry he respected the principle of his incarnation, true and real manhood, just as he did in the other spheres already considered.

This is not only interesting but is of fundamental importance in understanding and defending his true and proper humanity and so his true and proper Saviourhood. He was genuinely human and just as in his temptation he refused to be anything other than man, thus maintaining his oneness with us, so in the miraculous works by which his ministry was attested he also refused to be anything other than man. It is for this reason that the apostle Peter says of him, 'Jesus of Nazareth was a man accredited by God to you by miracles, wonders and signs, which God did among you through him, as you yourselves know' (Acts 2:22). Peter is saying that people knew that these great works were the immediate effects of divine power, and proofs that Jesus had been sent by God. The implication is that we too should make the same deduction. This is the reason why we are able to trace the Spirit's work in Christ, not merely in his powerful preaching ministry but in those great works and healing miracles with which it was accompanied.

Thus in his works as well as his words we see that his earthly ministry was carried through in the power of the Holy Spirit. Filled with the Holy Spirit in unlimited fulness the

Jesus we see in those great works is giving active demonstration that he is the Messiah, who had been forecast and foreshadowed in the Old Testament. An example of this is found, for instance, in the familiar words of the prophet Isaiah, 'Then will the eyes of the blind be opened and the ears of the deaf unstopped. Then will the lame leap like a deer, and the tongue of the dumb shout for joy' (Isaiah 35:5,6). Those works of Jesus of Nazareth, and more especially in this connection, his miracles of restoration and healing, are specifically messianic signs, such as had been clearly and explicitly intimated in many messianic prophecies of the Old Testament. One thing they were doing in his ministry was furnishing proof of the fulness of his anointing. In this way they were pointing back into the Old Testament predictions and so supporting his own explicit, if infrequent, messianic claims.

The purpose of the miracles

The question must be faced as to why the Lord Jesus did perform miracles. The easy answer, and the one which perhaps springs to mind for most people, is that he did this to help very needy folk. He hated sickness and had come into the world to show men that if they trusted in him then they need not be sick. Or, we think he wanted to show the world how compassionate he was, and to teach his disciples in all ages how caring they also must be in their ministry. Or, yet again, we believe that he wanted to undo the works of sin in men and ensure that they went on to live clean, pure, and healthy lives. Some even suppose that miracles were basically didactic, meant to teach moral lessons. They have been spoken about as parables of his power performed mainly so that men would understand what regeneration and true godliness could achieve in a poor, sin-sick world. They were, on this view, not much more than dramatic illustrations of moral and spiritual truths.

No doubt the miracles of healing do demonstrate the love and compassion of Jesus, and his abhorrence of what sin had done in the creation. He did aim to help people. He did want to teach men to trust him. But those facts do not adequately explain why Jesus worked those mighty miracles. The reasons lie beyond the point of anything so far mentioned. It is to examine the purposes behind the miracles that we now turn.

If there is one thing the Bible makes abundantly clear it is that Jesus did not come into this world just to exercise a kind of medical mission. To utilize bodily healing as the interpretative principle, and to make those miraculous cures the main objective of his redemptive work is to misjudge Christ and misrepresent his gospel in a very serious way. Such a thesis fails to do proper justice to the enormity and the majesty of the task he came to implement. Healthy bodies and happy homes, while important factors in themselves, by no means adequately interpret the essence of his ministry in this world.

In the interests of men's souls and of the glory of God's saving grace, ministers, preachers, and Christian workers must, today, be very plain on this point. Our Lord Jesus did not come into the world only to exercise a ministry of healing upon the bodies of men. Bodily healing, in a world under the curse of God, but yet the subject of his redemptive love, must never be considered as the prime and most important ministry of Christ or of God's grace. There are times and occasions when it quite clearly is not God's intention to heal bodily ailments and it is through illness, weakness, suffering, and ultimately death that God's people finally enter into that rest which awaits them in heaven.

It is a mistake to centre the gospel of grace around bodily healing or temporal well-being alone because its message is so much wider and deeper than what these represent. Similarly it is a mistake to interpret the miracles of Jesus only in terms of their actual, individual, and particular bodily benefit to the person concerned. That was involved, and the Lord Jesus never regarded that as unimportant because the individual was always important to him. But it must be understood that healing was not the most important thing in Jesus' ministry. By far the most important factor was the spiritual and eternal blessings with which he was able to bless and benefit those to whom he ministered. While he clearly sympathized with ill people and loved them very deeply and set out to help them, he had come to deal with the greater, even more ugly reality which underlay all suffering and illness — sin. He had come to redeem them from the penalty and power of sin.

There can be little doubt that Jesus was far more concerned to save men from the evil consequences of their sin than he was to save them from the pain of their bodily sickness. It was towards this greater, higher, purpose that his miracles were wrought. They were signs and proofs of who Jesus was, God's Messiah. They were signs authenticating his teaching as being special revelation from God to man. Nicodemus, the ruler who came to Jesus by night came for this very reason. 'Rabbi, we know you are a teacher who has come from God. For no-one could perform the miraculous signs you are doing if God were not with him' (John 3:2). They were the insignia of his deity, authenticating his claims to divine Sonship. Again and again the works of power are mentioned as the reason why, on one level, men put their trust in him. 'This, the first of his miraculous signs,' writes the apostle John, 'Jesus performed in Cana of Galilee. He thus revealed his glory, and his disciples put their faith in him' (John 2:11).

The miracles were tokens of his supreme command over nature and over the soul and body of man. The majority of them were acts of mercy and they have been seen as emblems of redemption. By the genuineness of the visible miracle that of the invisible miracle was confirmed to men. To regard them as ends in themselves is to do the greatest disservice to the teaching of the New Testament.

Blaspheming the Spirit

It was because the Pharisees accused him of casting out demons by the power of Beelzebub, the prince of demons, and because this was so obviously absurd that Jesus warned them, very solemnly, about the blasphemy against the Holy Spirit. The warning is significant because of the light that it sheds upon the relationship between the incarnate Son and the Spirit who indwelt him. Also, the warning itself is couched in such intensely impressive language, and is delivered with such solemn emphasis, that it throws the enormity of blasphemy against the Spirit into very bold relief. It not only names it as a sin but names it as sin for which there is no forgiveness at all. In fact it contains a double declaration about this sin being one for which there is no forgiveness.

The first of those declarations is general in character and contrasts this blasphemy with other classes, or species, of blasphemy. 'And so I tell you, every sin and blasphemy will be forgiven men, but the blasphemy against the Spirit will not be forgiven' (v.31). Dreadful as this is in itself, it is not all that Jesus had to say about it. The second thing he says is, if anything, more solemn still. 'Anyone who speaks a word against the Son of Man will be forgiven, but anyone who speaks against the Holy Spirit [literally, the Spirit of holiness, with a rather unususal emphasis on the holiness] will not be forgiven, either in this age or in the age to come' (v.32). Clearly this goes further than the earlier statement. It advances to a still more solemn assertion, and contrasts this sin specifically with blasphemy against the Son of Man. That makes it even more wicked than what must be in itself a terribly aggravated sin.

The cumulative effect of these two declarations is to isolate the sin of blasphemy against the Holy Spirit in a startling way as the only sin which is entirely and for ever incapable of pardon. In this latter thought we must not imagine that Jesus is teaching that other sins can be forgiven in eternity. That is simply not the contrast he is making. The entire burden of Scripture gives no countenance to such ideas. This fact of a sin for which there is no forgiveness has often distressed many people, usually people who already show every sign of trusting Christ and thus being true Christians. Here we see that, at the very least, it falls into a specific and definite category of sin. It is a sin committed only against the Holy Spirit.

For further elucidation of this particular point, let us return, briefly, to the two declarations of Jesus. The first statement is couched in very simple terms. 'Every sin and blasphemy [the combined terms helping to fasten attention on the sinfulness of blasphemy] will be forgiven men, but the blasphemy [highlighting the particular blasphemy he has in mind] against the Spirit will not be forgiven.' Blasphemy meant then just what it means now — insult to the divine majesty, deliberate and conscious offensive statements about God, and blasphemy of the Spirit is distinguished only as a particular instance of the more general sin.

To this simple statement there is linked a repetition which is much more than mere repetition. It clarifies rather than adds to what has been said. It instances a particular application of the general truth which has been stated, and does this in such a way as to drive home that truth with great force. It has all been voiced when it is said, 'Every blasphemy shall be forgiven except the blasphemy of the Spirit.' But it is all given a new sharpness and thrust when it is added: 'Even if anyone blasphemes the Son of Man, he shall be forgiven, but not if he blasphemes the very Spirit of holiness — no, not for ever.' To blaspheme the Son of Man, and yet to be forgiven, is to illustrate forgiveness at its most incredible reach. It is also to highlight by the sheer starkness of the contrast the total enormity of blaspheming the Spirit. The blasphemy which can know no forgiveness when even blasphemy against the Son of Man is forgiven, must be a sin of a fearsome nature.

From the contrast made, to speak against the Son of Man is to blaspheme against him; and that might be thought to be the very extremity of all sin. It is over against this very sin that the guilt of the unforgivable sin is to be gauged. The fact that the one is still within the limit of the forgivable while the other has passed utterly beyond it is the real measure of its horror. It is to be noted in passing, that Jesus uses the title 'Son of Man' which is the special indicator of his humanity and his Saviourhood. But alongside that and in perfect harmony with it he is asserting his deity as strongly as can be. Clearly this Son of Man does not regard himself as mere man. It is only because he is more than mere man that speaking a word against him is blasphemy.

In linking this with the ministry of the Spirit in the miracles of Jesus, Matthew helps with the age-old problem of what, precisely, the 'unforgivable sin' is. It involves speaking injurious and insulting words against the Holy Spirit. These Pharisees were evidently verging on this sin when they attributed the power of the Spirit, working in the fully anointed Saviour, to Satan, or Beelzebub.

How Jesus honoured the Spirit

While there may be a great deal which is beyond comprehension in this very difficult subject of the sin against the Holy Spirit, or the unforgivable sin, it does shed light on the extremely high views that Jesus held, and taught, as to the nature, person, and deity of the Holy Spirit. It reveals how precious to him the Spirit was. The Lord Jesus, and the Spirit who anointed and indwelt him with a plenitude fulness, share an infinite oneness and unity — a basal relationship which far surpasses mere affinity and harmony. They are two persons, but we must never forget that they are one God. Between them there is an infinite and ineffable love and their co-operation in this great work of redemption is expressive of the unified purpose of God, Father, Son, and Spirit, as they work each in his own sphere, but always in corporate harmony, for our salvation.

There is, perhaps, some significance to be attached to the fact that Jesus laid particular emphasis on the quality of holiness in the Spirit in the second of the two statements. It is extremely difficult for us to separate blasphemy of the Son of Man from blasphemy of that Holy Spirit by whom he wrought his great works of healing. We accept the distinction only because Jesus himself made it and made it so strongly. But in accepting it we only accentuate the difficulty of understanding precisely what the unpardonable sin is.

The emphasis on the Spirit's holiness may help us appreciate how utterly reversed the values of such a blasphemer have become. The guilt of this sin may also have something to do with the fact that it is committed against the agent and executor of Godhead in the sphere of the application of redemption. The Holy Spirit alone illumines men's minds and renews their hearts and unites them to Christ in a saving way. He works faith in men's hearts and the unpardonable nature of the sin has sometimes been connected with final impenitence and refusal to believe.

On this understanding, the sin would involve a deliberate, self-conscious suppression of the Spirit's work in sinners. It would issue in rejecting all the strivings, promptings, impressions, and convictions for which the Spirit is responsible. It seems to be peculiarly the sin of those who know in their minds what they should be, and what they should do, and yet despite that knowledge go on persistently in a Christless life. But when all the various possibilities have been looked at, the sin still cannot be exactly pinpointed. This suggests that the Lord mentioned it in order that it should be a beacon of warning to every hearer of the gospel. From a pastoral point of view, it is helpful to reflect that other scriptures dealing with forgiveness make it clear that anxiety over and fear of this particular sin are indicators that it has not been committed. The person incurring this guilt is unlikely, ever again, to have any real concern about spiritual things and especially about soul salvation.

Perhaps the fact that Jesus calls himself Son of Man in this particular situation also has a bearing on his assertion that blasphemy against himself is forgivable. As Son of Man he is the only Mediator between God and man, the only Saviour, and as such he is to undergo what might be supposed to be the ultimate blasphemy; men are going to crucify and kill him. But even this is going to be turned to their benefit. God has ordained that his death will redeem his people and finally undo the kingdom of darkness. It is, perhaps, well that we are not finally able to identify the unpardonable sin precisely. To know that it is possible, and that it relates to blaspheming the Spirit, should etch it into our minds as something to avoid. Let us honour the Holy Spirit of God, even as Christ himself did.

The issue which has been focused in this chapter, by whose power Jesus did his works, does not remain back there in the debates and discussions which took place in the Palestine of two thousand years ago. The polarization between the Pharisees' view and Jesus' own explanation of his works is still with us. Unbelief does not merely neglect Jesus, it rejects him. In order to do so it has to come to some judgement of him. There is really no escape for anyone in this matter. Either Jesus has come forth from God and deserves total allegiance, or we can hardly avoid declaring him possessed of the evil one.

To take Jesus seriously and to attempt to interpret his amazing works and his sweeping claims means those alternatives constantly staring us in the face; he is either the Son of God as he claimed, or his claim is itself a blasphemy. There is no other option. He is Saviour or deceiver.

9
The Death of Jesus

'How much more, then, will the blood of Christ, who through the eternal Spirit offered himself unblemished to God, cleanse our consciences from acts that lead to death, so that we may serve the living God!'
(Hebrews 9:14).

The death of Christ is the climax of his redemptive mission. The focus of Old Testament prophecy, as well as New Testament history, is on his death as the one great sacrifice for sin. It might be thought that here, if anywhere, there is no possibility of tracing the Spirit's presence or work in Christ. It is the Lord Jesus who alone is the Redeemer of God's people and who alone was incarnate, who could experience death and pay the ultimate price for sin. That this is his special, particular, personal work has already been emphasized. The entire gospel message centres around the fact that it was Christ, not the Holy Spirit, who 'died for our sins according to the Scriptures' (1 Corinthians 15:3). And yet, as the text makes clear, the Holy Spirit of God was involved at this point and had a ministry to exercise in the Saviour throughout his suffering and sin-bearing.

In the light of previous chapters, however, the presence, anointing, and work of the Spirit in the sufferings and death of Christ will come as no surprise. In incarnation the Son of God had taken his place as a true man; from that place nothing, not even the suffering and dying of Calvary could remove him. Indeed the fact that it is death which is involved here requires the Spirit's work as surely as in his other human experiences. Godhead and Deity do not suffer and are not subject to death, and on the other hand, human nature needs the Holy Spirit for every holy work. It is in our nature that the Son of God becomes, in a very unique and special sense, our sin-bearer. This reminds us that it is as man the Lord Jesus is anointed and filled with the Spirit beyond measure.

The sacrifice — and the power of the Spirit

This anointing means Jesus' drawing upon the divine resources through the Holy Spirit, and the Spirit's empowering him in every aspect of his mediatorial work. We have seen that it is at the crisis periods in the life of Jesus that the Spirit's presence is most clearly discernible. The cross and death of the Lord Jesus constitute the climactic, critical task of his entire ministry. If the text is understood of the Holy Spirit, then the issue is put beyond question; it was through the Holy Spirit that Christ offered himself to God. The trinitarian thrust inherent in the theme emerges yet again, providing a coherent background to the biblical doctrine of the atonement. It is not possible to look at the cross through the words of the text without being as deeply conscious of the Trinity as at Jordan. This sacrifice involved the three persons of the Godhead. It was the Son who was offered in the sacrifice, and he was offered through the Spirit, and his offering of himself was to the Father.

In the previous paragraph, the phrase 'understood of the Holy Spirit' is used. There has been, historically, a difference of opinion about the actual reference here. There have been theologians and expositors in almost every age who have interpreted the words 'eternal Spirit' as referring to the divine nature of Christ rather than to the Holy Spirit.

This school of thought has represented Christ as acting in, or through, his divine nature as the High Priest of God. In this capacity he must have something to offer and, of course, it holds that this 'something' was his human nature. There was a rather neat little saying which summarized the thought and captured the imagination: 'He offered his humanity on the altar of his deity.' But if we look at the text more carefully we see that by reading it in this way, we ultimately arrive at a tautology — a meaningless repetition of what is so clearly expressed in the words, 'offered himself'. This interpretation makes an unacceptable distinction between Christ's person and his divine nature, and encourages an unwarranted dividing of the person of Christ.

It is not the divine nature but the whole person who is priest; it is not the human nature that is offered as sacrifice, it is himself; all that he was, all that he had done. The above interpretation reverses the plain meaning of the text and runs counter to the theology of Christ's sacrifice of himself. This becomes clearer if we remember that the sacrifice of which it speaks was actually an offering right into death. It was because he was man that death could be real and possible for the Lord Jesus. Theologically the truth is that the Son offered himself to God in and by the *human* nature and not, as this interpretation urges, the divine nature. The sacrifice was made in the human nature filled, anointed, and strengthened by the Holy Spirit; hence, it was an offering of himself through the eternal Spirit.

There is no reason at all, either theologically or grammatically, for not accepting this statement at its plain face value. Within the framework of these chapters the theological as well as the grammatical considerations urge us to interpret the words in this simple, straightforward way. The opinions of two well-known and trustworthy expositors may be given here.

First of all, John Owen acknowledges that the text is sometimes taken as meaning the divine nature of Christ. Having granted that, and without rigidly excluding its possibility, he then says, 'But, on the other side, many learned persons, both of the ancient and modern divines, do judge that it is the person of the Holy Spirit that is intended' (*Works of John Owen*, Banner of Truth, 1965, vol.3, p.176). He then proceeds to give one of the clearest expositions we have of how the Holy Spirit was involved in the death of the cross, so that obviously this is the view he adopts himself.

Secondly, George Smeaton writes in the strongest terms against understanding the words in any other way but as referring to the Holy Spirit. 'The expression: "the eternal

Spirit,"* he writes, 'can only mean the Holy Spirit according to the usual acceptation of the term, — not the divine nature of Christ, as too many expositors have understood it. The meaning is, that the Son of God, moved and animated by the Holy Ghost, offered Himself without spot as an atoning sacrifice . . . To explain the text as if it described the divine nature as priest and the human nature as the sacrifice, is inadmissible. The WHOLE Person is priest and victim; for all done by either nature belongs to the Person' (*The Doctrine of the Holy Spirit*, p.132).

The real question at issue here is, whether as regards his human nature Christ chose to dispense with the resources of the Holy Spirit; or did he have the ordinary operation (in unlimited fulness, of course) of the Holy Spirit. We remind ourselves again of two principles which are fundamental to an understanding of the biblical teaching on the incarnation. First, God has so created human nature that without the Holy Spirit it can have no virtue or holiness. 'The shining-in of the Holy Spirit', writes Abraham Kuyper in this connection, 'is as essential to holiness as the shining of light into the eye is essential to seeing' (*The Work of the Holy Spirit*, p.103). Secondly, the incarnation meant that Christ would in *all things* be made like his brothers; he would be, and was a true man. His divine nature gave him no advantages in the matter of obedience, not even when it was obedience to death. He is paying the wages of sin and he is doing it as true man.

Applying those two principles to the question before us we see that Christ's human nature could not, at any moment, dispense with the constant 'inshining' of the Holy Spirit. Kuyper says — and even in translation it is beautifully expressed — 'As to the question, whether the Godhead of Christ did not support His humanity, we answer: Undoubtedly; but never independently of the Holy Spirit. We *faint* because we resist, grieve and repel the Holy Spirit. Christ was always victorious because His divinity never relaxed His hold upon the Holy Spirit in His humanity, but embraced Him and clave unto Him with all the energy of the Son of God' (ibid.).

Having clarified the words, and shown why they refer to

119

the Holy Spirit, we consider how he ministered to the Saviour in his sufferings. To pinpoint the central thrust of the text, and get a clear grasp of its teaching will help us appreciate more fully what it has to say about the role of the Spirit.

The sacrifice — and Christ's priestly activity

The focal point of the text concerns what Christ was doing in his death on the cross; he was offering himself. The word used is expressive of activity and, if one may use the term, even of employment. In his dying Christ was busily employed; he was fulfilling the greatest task ever accomplished in this world; he was putting away sin by 'the sacrifice of himself' (Hebrews 9:26). He was acting in the capacity of our great High Priest, appointed to the role by God the Father and anointed for it by God the Spirit.

It is easy to think of the death of the Lord Jesus Christ almost exclusively in terms of suffering and submissive enduring. This is natural, for these lie on the very surface of all the Gospel narratives. The immediate impact of the cross is to impress us with the terrible things done to him. However, the Bible does not leave matters there but goes on to interpret the entire sequence of events that led to his death as something done *by* him, as well as something done *to* him. Scripture will not allow us to think of him as completely passive in his death, nor as merely submitting to a series of events over which he had no control. The biblical emphasis is consistently on his participation in a momentous achievement.

This note of accomplishment was prominent in the prophetic predictions of Messiah's death. Isaiah for example says not only that Christ 'was numbered with the transgressors', but also that 'he poured out his life unto death' (Isaiah 53:12). It is the key theme in Christ's own teaching about his mission: 'The Son of Man did not come to be served, but to serve, and to give his life as a ransom for many' (Matthew 20:28). It couches at the heart of Paul's passionate proclamation of the cross: 'Christ', he says to the Ephesians, 'loved the church and gave himself up for her' (Ephesians 5:25). It is this aspect of the cross, and the priestly activity that was being

120

exercised upon it, that is in the forefront of what the text has to say about the death of Christ; he 'offered'.

The sacrifice — and the forces involved

There is a great deal of other, intense activity clustering around the events of the cross. Jesus was being made a victim. He was being made the object of very varied attention, and was coming under the pressures and influences of immensely potent physical, spiritual, and even eternal forces.

Men laid hold on Jesus. They were fiercely engaged in getting rid of the prophet of Nazareth, and their energy and thought — in some cases their craft and cunning — were directed towards his death. Peter was absolutely right when he said to the Jews and their leaders on the Day of Pentecost, 'And you, with the help of wicked men, put him to death by nailing him to the cross' (Acts 2:23).

More sinister forces were engaged in bringing about his death. The malignant power of evil was also participating in Christ's agony. Scripture tells us that it was Satan who motivated the traitor-disciple to the act of betrayal; as the cross came near, Jesus spoke to the Jews of the 'power of darkness' (Luke 22:53); the very first promise of a Saviour predicted that the hand of Satan should be in the cross (Genesis 3:15); the serpent was to bruise the heel of the promised seed.

Above all, the Father's hand and agency must be acknowledged in the death of Jesus. His eternal counsel and purpose had, in amazing mercy and love, set up the cross even before the foundations of the world were laid (Ephesians 1:4). He it was who, acting in the tribunal of eternal righteousness, represented all the holy interests of Deity when our Surety and Substitute, Jesus the Christ, stood at his bar in the place of the guilty. Paul tells us that it was God, the Sovereign Lord, that 'made him who had no sin to be sin for us' (2 Corinthians 5:21). It was the Father who called upon the sword of justice to smite the shepherd of the flock (Zechariah 13:7).

Scripture takes us behind the visible events of the cross and unveils all those forces at work in Christ's death; but it does

121

even more than that. It supports the emphasis of the text; despite the presence and power of all those other forces, Jesus himself was also active. Meek, gentle, obedient, willing, submissive — in his death Christ was all of those things, and each of them is seen in him here at its highest and best — but he was not inactive in his submission to the Father's will.

The truth lies in the very opposite direction. His obedience lay not only in mere acceptance but in assertive exertion. His giving of himself was not negative but positive. His offering of himself in sacrifice was carried through with all his heart and mind and soul. It was obedience given out of love to the Father and love to the lost. It was glad, whole-hearted obedience. Never was God worshipped in sacrifice as he was worshipped in this offering; nothing was withheld from him, but all was given in full understanding of what God is and what sin deserves. It is not merely that Christ was there, offering himself in death; the truth is far grander than that; there was nowhere else in all the reaches of the universe that he would rather be; nothing else he would prefer to be doing. This was his work, this was his will, this was his mission. He gave himself fully to all that it demanded. His own positive, powerful action is in exercise all the time; he 'offered himself'.

The sacrifice — and the Old Testament background

This word 'offered' belongs to a very highly technical vocabulary; it is part of the language of Old Testament sacrifice and priestly activity. It was used of the lambs, and the doves, and the animals that people brought to the priest that he might 'offer' them for the expiation and atonement of their sins. The priest then took the animal, and in accordance with the legislation laid down by God for acceptable sacrifice, the animal was 'offered' at the altar. Life was taken, because the price of sin is, always, the forfeiting of life. Life was offered, and the offered life was accepted as substitute for the person.

This substitution was accepted in the Old Testament order, not because animal life was equated with the immortal life of man, but to teach that sin leads to death and, above all, that

God was going to provide a substitute. Unlike the pagan nations with their many rites of human sacrifice, Israel was forbidden the sacrificial slaying of people made in the image of God; she was taught that even human death was no ransom for human sin; and yet, through animal sacrifice she learned the twin truths of the sinfulness of sin, and the pardoning mercy of God. Supremely, the sacrifices pointed forward to the laying down of a life that was infinitely more precious than that of men — the sacrifice of Christ himself. In this way, and against that background, the Jewish believers to whom this Epistle was addressed would interpret the text. In offering himself on the cross, Christ was fulfilling the office of our Priest. He was making one, great sacrifice for sins for ever. There would never need to be another.

Priesthood implies representation. A priest acts on behalf of others. He mediates between men and God. It is of the Old Testament priesthood and sacrifice that this very writer is speaking when he says, 'Every high priest is selected from among men and is appointed to represent them in matters related to God, to offer gifts and sacrifices for sins' (Hebrews 5:1). Representing Israel, the priest was taken from Israel. Men were taught to look for a mediator from among men. This prefigured Messiah taking our nature, our Priest being one of us.

If staff in an engineering plant, or shipyard, or workshop wish to be represented with the Management, and have their needs met and rights promoted, then its members choose a delegate and present him as their spokesman. They find him, not in the ranks of Management but on the factory floor. This means that their representative knows their working conditions, their difficulties, and so on. He knows the circumstances and realities facing the workers as Management never can, by experience. He understands their thinking and sympathizes with their needs because he is one of them. This is why he is so suitable as the workers' representative. As far as they are concerned, he is 'one of themselves'. He will plead their cause from the strong position of personal experience.

That is precisely what is required in a priest. It is what every

Christian believer has in Christ, a High Priest who shares his nature, who was here in this world and lived under the same conditions, and experienced the same hardships as does every one of his followers. These chapters have emphasized again and again that Jesus was truly man. He knew what it was to 'live by faith' in God. He knew what it was to be dependent on and to seek the presence of the Father in prayer. He knew what it was to have the indwelling and the power and the enlightening of the Holy Spirit. It should greatly comfort our hearts that the Spirit was there ministering to the man Christ Jesus even in his atoning and offering of himself upon the cross. Every Old Testament priest was anointed with oil for the offering of sacrifice. Our High Priest was anointed with the Holy Spirit as he offered himself in 'one sacrifice for sins' (Hebrews 10:12).

The sacrifice — and Christ's personal offering

In addressing the question what it was that Christ offered, we shall gain a better understanding of the Spirit's ministry to the Saviour in his priestly work. Christ was not merely passive and submissive, but very active and resolute as High Priest; he not only suffered; he offered. He offered in suffering, and he suffered in offering. He went on in the face of all opposition until the task was complete and he could cry out, for heaven and earth to hear, 'It is finished' (John 19:30).

The text tells us what Christ offered. It was 'himself'. It was the person of the Son of God, who became incarnate and who was 'found in appearance as a man' (Philippians 2:8). This human nature never had any separate identity, or personal existence, far less any personal experience, except as it was united to the person of the Son. This is the outstanding feature about this death; it is experienced by the person who is the Son of God, who is 'very God of very God'. In human nature he 'tastes' death, and in doing so, he pays the price of sin. At the cross the words of John the Baptist assume a reality of awful proportion: 'Look, the Lamb of God, who takes away the sin of the world!' (John 1:29). He is not only the Priest who offers, he is the Lamb who suffers.

124

It was necessary that Christ be human in order to be able to sacrifice himself. It was also necessary that he be God in order that the infinite guilt of sin might be borne, and its punishment removed for ever. The sacrifice offered was the sacrifice of the God-man. Christ has two natures but is one person; that person suffers and dies at Calvary. The experience undergone was that of death, and although the death of a true man, it was also the experience of the Son of God.

An ancient rule of theology comes to our aid here: whatever is predicated of either nature, is to be predicated of the person. Men had died before. But this death is unique because Jesus did not deserve to die. In the whole history of a universe governed by a righteous God, this is the first and only time a sinless man had been visited with a sinner's punishment. He can be so visited, righteously, only because he is there in the place of the guilty; he can be so visited, practically, only because he is sinless. Otherwise, he would have needed for himself the blessing which he came to confer on others. Only one without sin could be made sin.

From the biblical perspective there is a sense in which the death of this man is identical with the death of other men. It is, basically, the separation of soul and body; a profound disruption of personality from the norm. But from the same perspective this death is markedly different from every other which has ever taken place. Once death had severed the bond between soul and body it came across another bond which it was unable to disrupt; that was the bond between Christ's divine and human natures. The sword of death could not prevail against the divine person and so was unable to divide what had been linked in incarnation. This meant that, in the very midst of death, there was life which death could not touch.

The Son of God was still alive, and the human body which he had taken was still his; so was the human soul. They were separated in death but yet each was still united to the person of the Son of God. This truth has been put as follows: With one divine hand the Son of God, as it were, held his soul in the presence of his Father, while with the other he held his body in the grave; and so, although separated from one another in death they were still united in his divine person. Here too, the action was Christ's own. Life was not wrested from him; rather, he yielded it up himself. Death was peculiarly of his own volition. 'Father, into your hands I commit my spirit' (Luke 23:46). He was not powerless, as other men are in death, but powerful. He had taught his disciples that this was how it would be: 'I lay down my life — only to take it up again. No-one takes it from me, but I lay it down of my own accord. I have authority to lay it down and authority to take it up again. This command I received from my Father' (John 10:17,18).

An illustration may help at this point. If a person pulls a sword out of its sheath and holds sword in one hand and scabbard in the other, they are, although separate, still united through that person. That illustrates, even if dimly, what took place in the death of Christ. Death did its worst, and yet death was conquered. That is why the great theologian, John Owen, could write a book on the atonement and entitle it *The Death of Death in the Death of Christ*.

The sacrifice — and the purity of its presentation

The text emphasizes the spotlessness and purity, the sinlessness and perfection of Christ in his sacrifice. It is in this area, specifically, that theologians have tended to trace the ministry of the Spirit in the transaction. 'The Spirit', writes Smeaton, 'rendered Him an unspotted sacrifice. The Spirit discovered to Him the inflexible claims of God as well as inflamed Him with such love to man and zeal for God as prompted Him to go forward in spite of every hindrance, pain, and difficulty, to effect the world's redemption, and thus fitted Him as man for His work' (*Doctrine of the Holy Spirit*, p.132).

Many of the Old Testament sacrifices were actually offered through fire, and sometimes their acceptance was intimated by their being burned up with a fire which came down from heaven. Fire was a symbol, not merely of God's presence by the Spirit, but of purity and holiness. In this way the action of

126

the Holy Spirit was vividly represented by the holy fire by which the sacrifices were consumed. The flames were the symbol of how the Spirit would be at Calvary to devote and consecrate the priestly sacrifice to be offered there.

It is the apostle John who records the high priestly prayer of Christ on the very eve of his suffering and how, praying for his followers, he said, 'For them I sanctify myself, that they too may be truly sanctified' (John 17:19). As far as inherent holiness was concerned the Lord Jesus was perfect, so he obviously is not speaking of sanctifying himself in that sense. He was in fact speaking of his death, and his devotion to the task it involved and its effects upon us. This is confirmed when we read, 'And by that will we have been made holy [sanctified] through the sacrifice of the body of Jesus Christ once for all' (Hebrews 10:10). This dedication of himself was his first action as sacrificing Priest, and it was performed in the power of the Holy Spirit in him.

The sacrifice — and its perfect achievement

His offering through the grace of the eternal Spirit ensured the holiness and purity of his already sinless sacrifice. All that was embraced in this offering was enhanced by the dignity of Christ's own person and effected through the strengthening grace of the Spirit. Love to men and compassion to sinners, in the human heart of the Lord, were in their highest exercise throughout this Spirit-anointed offering. This love is often mentioned in relation to the offering: 'who loved me and gave himself for me', said the apostle Paul (Galatians 2:20). Love to the Father, passionate concern for his glory in the salvation of sinners, and zeal for his justice and holiness filled the soul of the man Christ Jesus. Faith, trust, obedience, and submission were all being exercised in the purity of perfection and, being graces of the Spirit in the human heart, and Christ being true man, this was one area of the Spirit's ministry to the Saviour as he bore our sins.

It is also the case that the Spirit was strengthening what was true, and therefore frail, human nature. Tremendous forces were being exerted against him; sin was being laid upon him;

wrath was being borne by him; the felt presence of the Father was taken from him. The weight of the curse and the experience of eternal death brought with them a banishment and dereliction none can ever appreciate. In all this, he was filled by the Spirit without measure, and so 'through the eternal Spirit offered himself . . . that we may serve the living God!'

Love to the Father, love to his people, and that love sustained at its most intense level throughout his suffering and offering fills his atoning achievement with fragrance for the Father and comfort for us. There can be no doubt that the spiritual pain of being accounted as a sinner, and coming into the closest, yet sinless contact with our guilt was an unspeakable agony for him. As Augustine put it, 'The sufferings of his soul, were the soul of his suffering.' There was absolutely no reluctance in the heart or soul of this Priest as he met our obligations and paid our debt. Rather he, 'for the joy set before him endured the cross, scorning its shame' (Hebrews 12:2).

This is the only place in Scripture where the Spirit is spoken of as the eternal Spirit and, the two words, 'eternal' and 'holy', in Greek being quite similar (*aioniou* and *hagiou*), some have thought that perhaps a slip on the part of some scribe accounts for the unusual title. All the evidence is against that, however, and there could be no more suitable title for the Spirit, in the work he was doing here, than this one which he himself inspired. Eternal issues were being settled in the death of Jesus. Eternal wrath was being experienced; eternal punishment was being endured; eternal salvation was being secured; eternal death was being faced; eternal justice was being satisfied; eternal love was being demonstrated; and it is altogether appropriate that the one who sustains the Saviour throughout should be the eternal Spirit.

In this hour eternity had burst into time. The 'throne of God and of the Lamb' was being safeguarded and established for ever. It was the eternal Spirit alone who could fathom all the factors involved, and who could, in some sense, company with the Redeemer on this lonely, lofty peak of redemptive achievement. The executor, the perfector of all the works of Trinity is here. He is here not to suffer or die or redeem — that is the work of the incarnate Son alone; the Spirit is here ensuring that the atoning work of the Son is also brought through to perfect, triumphant conclusion. It was in this way that the manhood of the Saviour could be carried through such unutterable suffering and unutterable anguish to the place where he shouted in triumph, 'It is finished', and thus signalled his victory. His death was not merely a dying, it was a doing. And it was the grandest doing of all his redemptive work for us.

The sacrifice — and its effectiveness

Before leaving this subject of atonement, let us recall the main thrust of the text. It compares and contrasts the sacrifice of Christ with the Old Testament sacrifices by which it was prefigured. The two are contrasted in order to highlight the superiority of Christ's finished work. Hebrew converts may lose the elaborate ritual of Temple sacrifice, but they gain the reality of which the ritual was only the shadow. It is not merely better; it is superlatively and eternally better. There is that striking 'How much more' label attached to every aspect of Christ's work, advertising its superiority over all the ceremonies of the old order. How much more perfect; how much more personal; how much more precious; how much more costly; how much more effective. How much more comforting for us to have the finished work to review, than only its coming to anticipate.

The text makes it clear that the sacrifice has a twofold application. The blood of Christ viewed as shed, renders the salvation of the sinner consistent with the perfections of the divine character. The same blood, viewed as sprinkled on the believing sinner, cleanses from all sin. The second depends on the first. The blood must be shed in order to be sprinkled. These two great spiritual realities are encompassed in the text. Sinners can be saved through believing in Jesus, and God can be just in saving them. The Spirit's ministry in the Son ensures that both these ends are realized.

10
The Resurrection of Jesus

*'He was put to death in the body but made alive
by the Spirit'* (1 Peter 3:18).

Previous chapters have been dealing with our Lord in what
theologians have called the 'state of humiliation'. That is a
fitting description of his incarnate life and his earthly
ministry. We have seen how the Holy Spirit continually worked in the Saviour as he descended the various steps of his
humiliation, a process that began on the shining throne and
took him down into the death of the cross and the darkness of
the tomb. The question must now be faced as to whether the
Spirit had a ministry in the steps of Christ's exaltation which
took him from the tomb back to the throne. His exaltation involved resurrection, ascension, and session on the right hand
of the 'Majesty on high'. Here too, Scripture indicates the in-
volvement of the Holy Spirit and so we shall look at the resurrection and then at the ascension as the two final crisis events
of Christ's work. In doing so we shall see again the presence
and power of the Holy Spirit.

Humiliation and exaltation converge in resurrection

The eternal Son of God entered upon his saving mission, and
his state of humiliation began, when his human nature was
conceived in the womb of the virgin Mary. The opposite process of exaltation as Mediator began when his body and soul
were reunited in resurrection.

Scripture links an empty tomb, angelic messengers, surprised disciples, and a risen Saviour in a way that marks resurrection as the beginning of his mediatorial glory. His resurrection body was human not only in appearance but was a true, though risen, human body. Nor was his human nature 'deified' by resurrection. It was human nature still. The elements reunited in resurrection were the body and soul of the man Christ Jesus. Peter states that this was a miracle of the Spirit, that the reconstitution took place by the power of the Spirit; 'he was . . . made alive by the Spirit'.

It was not a human person he took into union with himself but, rather, the constituent elements of human personality. That specific human nature, consisting in the union of a rational soul and a real, flesh and blood body, was never the human nature of any other but the person of the Son of God. When we encounter the Jesus of the New Testament the person involved is that of the eternal Son. This feature of the incarnation has to be emphasized because the nature of the person incarnated determines the nature of the person resurrected and exalted. The resurrection is so great a miracle that it taxes the belief of some. But it must be remembered that the incarnation is a far greater miracle. Accept the fact that Jesus really is God the Son, and the resurrection is seen from a new perspective. Seen thus, non-resurrection would be far more surprising than even the empty tomb.

Atonement and exaltation

It is necessary to trace where Christ's state of humiliation ends and where that of exaltation begins. There is a school of thought which speaks of the state of humiliation ending the moment Christ stepped over the doorstep of death. In support of the thesis that his exaltation also began then, they have two suggestions.

One is that from the moment of death he was out of the hands of wicked men. His body was requested by Joseph of Arimathea, a member of the Jewish Council, and against every likelihood — for those killed under the Roman law of capital punishment were normally buried at the foot of the cross — Pilate consented to the unusual request, and Joseph was given the body. Assisted by another leader of the Jews, Nicodemus, Joseph took the body of Jesus down from the cross and placed it in a rock-hewn garden tomb, perhaps his own, thus providing the sort of burial that only a rich man could afford. It has been put like this: 'His exaltation began when his blessed body which had been broken and in which he had suffered was given the grave of a rich man.' The idea is attractive, but the fact of the matter is that he was still in a state of death and that was, and always will be, the lowest state of humiliation.

Another factor enlisted in support of this idea is that, with death actually experienced, sin's debt was fully paid, his mission was complete, salvation achieved. Scripture does, of course, forge a strong link between atonement and exaltation, and Christ's presence on heaven's throne is the ultimate intimation of God's acceptance of his work and its perfection. All that is perfectly true but it is the resurrection itself that is one of the chief tokens of God's acceptance of the person and work of the Saviour.

Resurrection initiates exaltation

Those factors mentioned have to be borne in mind. At the very least they cast rays of splendid light into the sufferings of the cross and the darkness of the grave. But despite these gleams of the light of God penetrating the state of death in which he was held, and despite the theologians who believe that his exaltation began as soon as his death was accomplished, it is preferable to say that his exaltation begins only on the edge of the grave; on that edge over which he emerges into his resurrection life.

The indications are that it is then he leaves the state of humiliation behind him and begins to enter into his mediatorial glory. He is the same Jesus who went to the cross; and yet, he is noticeably different. There is an aura of kingly achievement and heavenly authority about his post-resurrection appearances and words that is eloquent of this standing. Certainly, only then is his triumph evident and manifested. The facts that, as the *Shorter Catechism* puts it, he remained 'under the power of death for a time', and that Son though he was, he allowed the bands of death to hold him, are all indicators that while his body was in the grave, and in separation from his soul, he was still, however victorious thus far, in a state of humiliation. Only when he breaks the bars of death and emerges out of the grave does exaltation really begin.

Resurrection and not resuscitation

The resurrection of the Lord Jesus is different, uniquely different, from every other raising from the dead recorded in the Scriptures. Men speak of the resurrection of Lazarus and the resurrection of the son of the widow of Nain and the resurrection of Jairus' daughter, and so on. These were not resurrections in the sense in which Christ was resurrected. Christ's resurrection is different in this way. He went into the grave from the same side, so to speak, from which we must also go into the grave; but he came out of the grave on the far side, having passed through death and having finished with the grave for ever. That is resurrection in its proper sense and meaning.

In the instance of the young man, the widow of Nain's son, Jesus touched the bier on which the body lay, and he gave the kingly command, 'Young man . . . get up!' and the young man who had been bowed down in death was lifted up again. But the very moment he was lifted up, just because he was still in sinful human nature, and part of the human condition in a fallen world is death, he began to bow back towards death again. The moment he was brought to life, the processes which lead on to death were back at work once more. The time would come when he would, yet again, be carried out of his town to the burying place.

Not so with the Lord Jesus — quickened by the Spirit, his human life has the quality of eternity in it. 'The power of an endless life' is how the Epistle to the Hebrews expresses the authority of the priesthood which the man Christ Jesus exercised after the resurrection from the dead. When that Epistle talks about the power of an endless life, it is not the life of the

133

eternal Son that is meant. That always was endless and could not be anything else. This is the life of the Son in human nature, the Mediator, the Redeemer, our great High Priest — he is made alive with the power of eternal life — that is resurrection; it is life which dies no more, is no longer subject to the processes that lead to death. The others mentioned were, at best, resuscitation. Lazarus, the little girl, the young man, they all have some day to bow down in death and go into the grave. The resurrection of believers will be by the same Spirit, through the same power, into the same quality of life unceasing.

The preserving power of the Spirit

Scripture implies that even when Jesus was in a state of death there was a ministry of the Spirit in his human person. For example David says, 'My body also will rest secure, because you will not abandon me to the grave, nor will you let your Holy One see decay' (Psalm 16: 9,10). John Owen says of this: 'It is the body of Christ which is here called "the Holy One," as it was made a "holy thing" by the conception of it in the womb by the power of the Holy Ghost' (*Works*, p.180). Peter, preaching on the Day of Pentecost, reminds the Jews that the tomb and dust of David the psalmist were with them still and says that these words were spoken of a descendant; 'Seeing what was ahead, he spoke of the resurrection of the Christ, that he was not abandoned to the grave, nor did his body see decay' (Acts 2:31).

Obviously there was no sense in which the ordinary processes of corruption invaded the body of Jesus. That was not because he was embalmed and robed in a great variety of precious spices. It was because of a special ministry of the Holy Spirit to a body that had always been perfect, although truly human. The Holy Spirit who ensured that this body would be 'holy, blameless, pure' in its conception in the womb of the virgin Mary, ensured by his ministry that it would be kept holy, harmless, and undefiled while he was in the womb of the grave. In addition to the fact that this was the body of the Son, there is a very real sense in which, once

134

death had taken place, sin's debt had been fully paid and so there was to be no more suffering, no more downgrading, even for the body of the Son.

It would seem that his greatest suffering took place while darkness covered the face of the earth. It was then, out of the place of God's desolating curse, that he cried to God in the anguished question, '*Why?*' That cry came from the place of desertion and dereliction — the place where God shows no favour and only his curse is felt; but it would seem that the Saviour had already been released from that when he cried, 'It is finished.'

Why then did he remain in the state of death and under its power for three days? In the ninth chapter of the Epistle to the Hebrews an analogy was established between the annual Day of Atonement in the Old Testament order, and the death of the Lord Jesus. It will help to look at certain elements of that contrast for the old order has a light to shed on the new. Some of the main events which happened on the Day of Atonement must be given their due weight.

On the Day of Atonement the high priest went into the holy of holies, and he could only go in bearing the basin of sacrificial blood in his hands. This represented a life forfeited, the penalty for sin. As he entered the inner sanctuary there was, outside, the immense gathering of the congregation of Israel. Every soul in it was filled with eager anticipation. This was the occasion of the most solemn and sober worship they knew. It was the greatest of all their annual days of religious observance. The high priest took blood and sprinkled it on the mercy seat over which was the Shekinah glory, that token of the presence of God in the midst of his people. He sprinkled the ark of the covenant and the horns of the altar and purified these things; 'It was necessary, then, for the copies of the heavenly things to be purified with these sacrifices, but the heavenly things themselves with better sacrifices than these' (Hebrews 9:23).

This ceremony taught Israel a solemn and emphatic lesson about sin, holiness, and atonement. 'But only the high priest entered the inner room, and that only once a year, and never

135

without blood, which he offered for himself and for the sins the people had committed in ignorance' (Hebrews 9:7). What the high priest was doing was bringing the symbol of death accomplished into the holy of holies. In doing so, he was fulfilling a demand of the divine justice, and recognizing a principle of the divine government — 'the soul who sins is the one who will die' (Ezekiel 18:4), and 'without the shedding of blood [death] there is no forgiveness' (Hebrews 9:22). The comparison and contrast being drawn, and the lessons about the death and work of our Lord Jesus now become evident.

In the gospel of the cross, with its suffering and death, our great High Priest is sacrificing himself; he is himself the Priest, himself the victim. The sacrifice, completed and manifested in physical death, embraced within it eternal death also because he was the eternal Son. 'Christ did not enter a man-made sanctuary that was only a copy of the true one; he entered heaven itself, now to appear for us in God's presence' (Hebrews 9:24).

Christ's entry into heaven may be considered from another perspective. When he said to the thief on the cross, 'Today, you will be with me in paradise', what he meant was that he would be with him in the actual presence of God, enjoying salvation and fellowship with himself, as the living, human Jesus; there would be in heaven the soul of the Saviour and the soul of the sinner; the soul of the Redeemer, and the soul of the redeemed.

The analogy of Hebrews nine suggests that when the soul of Jesus appeared in paradise, or in the presence of God, it did so in separation from his body, that is, in the state of death. The presence of his soul without his body was prefigured by the ceremonial appearance of the high priest in the holy of holies bearing sacrificial blood. When Jesus entered the presence of God as our High Priest he did so 'not without blood'. That entry could be made only when blood had been shed. Christ entered having laid down his life. His soul, separated from the body, certified death as accomplished; signalized actual death just as clearly as does blood. At the same time there is a wonder that we must not forget, for his human soul, even in death, was still united to his divine person. This was demonstrated earlier by the illustration of the sword and the scabbard.

If this interpretation is correct, it will answer the question of theologians, When did this appearing in the presence of God for us take place? When did our High Priest sprinkle the real heavenlies? Many have maintained it was at his ascension. But Hebrews nine firmly links death and entry together, indicating coincidence between them. If that is so, then our High Priest could go in with all the insignia, and the reality of death about him, his soul being present in paradise, while his body still lay in the tomb.

What a comfort to know that it was as our High Priest that he went into the presence of God, and ministered there, taking with him the evidence of atonement and completed sacrifice. In order that his people might never doubt the reality of his presence there, or the achievement of his death, he remained 'under the power of death for a time', and only for a time. Death could not hold him.

One more feature of the annual Day of Atonement may be mentioned in direct relation to the resurrection of Christ. While the high priest was ministering in the holy of holies there was great anxiety amongst the assembled people of Israel. They were anxiously awaiting his reappearance. Only then would they know that the sacrifice had been accepted, that God had been propitiated, that sin's price had been both paid and accepted. On the emergence of the priest, he was greeted with a great shout of joy.

On the analogy which Hebrews institutes, this reappearance of the priest and the joy of the people, may be taken as symbolizing the resurrection of the Lord Jesus and the stunned, surprised joy that his rising brought to his disciples. We must not underestimate that. They were a transformed little band. It has been well said that only the resurrection can explain the existence of the church. It changed defeated men into burning, passionate evangelists who would spare nothing, not even life itself, to spread the good news of a risen Saviour.

Raised from the dead in the power of the Spirit

In Scripture the resurrection is sometimes attributed to the Father, sometimes to the Holy Spirit, and sometimes to the Son himself. But Scripture tells us the order in which God works — from the Father, through the Son, by the Spirit. From this point of view, it is true that the Father's power was in the actual accomplishment of the resurrection, and it is true that the Son himself was active in it, but both were exercising their power through the executive of the works of Godhead, by the agency of the Holy Spirit; the dead Lord was quickened into resurrection life by the Spirit.

This is the teaching of the text. As was the case in Hebrews 9:14 and the words 'through the eternal Spirit', some commentators have taught that the 'Spirit' referred to here, refers to his own divine nature. This seems a strained interpretation. It is, in fact, an expedient to which we need not resort in explaining the text. The tenor of its teaching, when understood of the Holy Spirit, accords well with the doctrines of creation, incarnation as well as that of resurrection. Such a man as John Owen accepted this view of it as have most translators of the New Testament.

That the Spirit's power was the agency through which Godhead raised the Lord's body is taught elsewhere. Owen says, 'To the same purpose we are instructed by the apostle in Romans 8:11, "If the Spirit of him that raised up Jesus from the dead dwell in you, he that raised up Christ from the dead shall also quicken your mortal bodies by his Spirit that dwelleth in you;" — "God shall quicken our mortal bodies also by the same Spirit whereby he raised Christ from the dead;" for so the relation of the one work to the other requires to be understood' (*Works*, vol. 3, p.182). Owen also cites Ephesians 1:17-20; Romans 1:4; and 1 Timothy 3:16, as teaching that the resurrection of Christ was accomplished by the power of the Holy Spirit.

It is highly significant that this should be so. In it there is a complete fitness. The same one who imparts life to the believer, who quickened the Christian out of the death and corruption of sin, and brought him into newness of life in union with Christ, the same blessed Spirit quickened our Lord out of death, made him alive. The one who had been there at the incarnation, when the union between divinity and humanity was formed in the person of Jesus, the same one is there at resurrection, when the bond between soul and body, severed by the sword of death, is being reunited never to be broken again.

The resurrection body of the Lord Jesus in itself makes a very interesting and fruitful subject of study. For example, it is quite clear that his resurrection body was the very same body which was laid in the tomb, and yet, that in many ways it was different. Our Lord, for one thing, never described himself after his resurrection as 'flesh and blood' — he says, 'flesh and bones'. That has some significance. It may have something to do with the fact that blood was shed as the price of sin. But the resurrection body was so closely identified with what it had been before death, that the risen Lord could eat with his disciples; and at the same time have wounds in his hands and in his side which would normally be quite inconsistent with bodily health and life. This body could pass through walls. It could defy the normal laws of physics as we think of them. He could appear at will and he could disappear at will. In this body he lived for forty days on earth, and ministered to people. His care and love and compassion had not changed; in many ways, he was the same Jesus; 'It is I myself' (Luke 24:39).

There is an almost unnoticed but powerful side-effect of the energy involved in and unleashed through the resurrection. Perhaps it is eloquent also of the presence and power of the Holy Spirit in his raising. We are told in Matthew 27 that 'the bodies of many holy people who had died were raised to life. They came out of the tombs, and after Jesus' resurrection they went into the holy city and appeared to many people' (Matthew 27:52,53). It would seem that as the Holy Spirit raised the eternal Son out of death there had to be some restraint on the graves of the saints as well. But the restraint was not total. The power of resurrection brought many of them out, firstfruits from the dead.

The body of his resurrection was the same and yet it was different. There was complete continuity and yet there was immense disparity between the pre- and post-resurrection condition. It holds interest for the Christian because it is the body on which the resurrection body of believers is to be patterned. In the resurrection bodies of the saints there will also be identity and discontinuity.

Paul writes on this subject and says, 'But someone may ask, "How are the dead raised? With what kind of body will they come?" . . . The body that is sown is perishable, it is raised imperishable; it is sown in dishonour, it is raised in glory; it is sown in weakness, it is raised in power; it is sown a natural body, it is raised a spiritual body . . . And just as we have borne the likeness of the earthly man so shall we bear the likeness of the man from heaven' (1 Corinthians 15:35, 42-44,49). What the Holy Spirit accomplished in the Saviour will have its complement and completion in every believer.

11
The Ascension of Jesus

'Exalted to the right hand of God, he has received
from the Father the promised Holy Spirit and has
poured out what you now see and hear' (Acts 2:33).

The ascension of the Lord Jesus Christ was the final step in his exaltation. To disregard it in our study of the Holy Spirit in the life of the Lord, would be to neglect the necessary link between his resurrection from among the dead, his reappearance amongst his disciples, and the outpouring of the Holy Spirit on the Day of Pentecost. Those are linked as cause and effect. His appearance among the disciples was the result of resurrection, the giving of the Spirit at Pentecost the result of his ascension. The text that heads this chapter links the work of the Spirit in the church with the presence of Christ on the throne. The apostle John confirms that order from the negative point of view when he reports of an early stage in Jesus' ministry, 'Up to that time the Spirit had not been given, since Jesus had not yet been glorified' (John 7:39). This glorification took place at Jesus' ascension.

The ascension — a real, bodily entrance to heaven

It is a sad reflection on attitudes to the gospel that we need to insist upon the actual historic fact of the ascension of the risen Jesus into the heavenly places. If the resurrection is denied, then of course there is no ascension. If on the other hand, the resurrection is established firmly as a fact, a message, and an experience that have shaped Christian belief and Christian behaviour for two thousand years, then it is equally certain that the raised Jesus ascended into heaven.

141

The resurrection body of Jesus had substantial reality. It could be observed, touched, and handled. That is the picture conveyed by the New Testament witness to the resurrection. One implication of this is very obvious; if Jesus' resurrection body had substantiality, it must also have had locality. It must have occupied its own specific space and had actual spatial relationships. That being so, all our normal experience and knowledge tell us that ascension into heaven meant not only a *state* of exaltation but a *place* of exaltation. It was not merely a body which ascended into heaven however, it was the *man* Christ Jesus. Sometimes people tend to speak of the ascended Lord as though his incarnation is now over. That is not so. Ascended into the midst of heaven's throne; exalted there with great glory on the 'right hand of the Majesty in heaven', he is still in human nature, still true man. He has not ceased to be man any more than Abraham, Moses, and Elijah have ceased to be men because they are in heaven. In fact, the presence of Jesus of Nazareth in heaven is more complete than that of any human there but Enoch and Elijah.

The actual ascension was a visible 'upgoing' from the earth, and a bodily leaving of the little group of people who were with him. It was, no matter how incomprehensible to their minds, an actual and observable event for those people. He was taken from them. They saw him go. Scripture speaks of 'the day he was taken up to heaven, after giving instructions through the Holy Spirit to the apostles he had chosen. After his suffering, he showed himself to these men and gave many convincing proofs that he was alive. He appeared to them over a period of forty days and spoke about the kingdom of God' (Acts 1:23). He took the disciples out to a mountain in Galilee and there, 'he was taken up before their very eyes, and a cloud hid him from their sight' (Acts 1:9).

That was the way the ascension appeared to men. It was vivid, real, actual. They could never forget it. It transformed their perspective on life and they lived out their days in the consciousness of the ascension kingship of Jesus. The motto of their days and their labour from that time on was 'Jesus is Lord.'

The Holy Spirit and the glorified Saviour

What was the ministry of the Spirit in this process? Even in his resurrection state, Jesus' work was being performed by the power of the Holy Spirit. He had not been thrust aside in any way. Not only was he the mover and energizer in the resurrection, but he continued to fill the risen Jesus 'without limit' and to be the agent of his purposes for the disciples. Jesus' ascension took place only after forty days. The leading feature of those days appears to have been teaching the disciples, and this process went on until the day he was taken up to heaven.

There is an emphasis also on the way in which the ascending Lord was taken from their view; he was watched until he was caught away in a cloud. There is one highly significant usage of the word 'cloud' in Scripture. It denotes the glory, or the glorious presence, of God.

As the children of Israel came out from their years of bondage in Egypt and took their journey into the desert, the presence of God was manifested in a luminous pillar of cloud by day and a pillar of fire by night. A pillar of fire is perhaps not the best translation, for it was a pillar of 'glowing brightness' in the dark. Again, it was a cloud that verified and manifested God's presence in the Temple as it overshadowed the mercy seat. The Lord Jesus was surrounded by, or caught into, a bright cloud on the Mount of Transfiguration which caused his divine glory to shine through his humanity so that even his clothes became white and glistening. It was called the Shekinah cloud, and was the awe-inspiring symbol of Jehovah's presence. As the Lord Jesus ascended, this was probably the cloud that came down and caught him out of sight. There would certainly still be a presence and ministry of the Holy Spirit in the man Christ Jesus at that glorious moment.

All that we have seen so far about the ministry of the Spirit in human nature constrains belief that the Son was still filled and indwelt by the Spirit in his ascension into heaven. Abraham Kuyper draws out the inferences from the general teaching of the Bible with crisp logic and language. He writes, 'According to Scripture, the Holy Spirit belongs to our nature as the light to the eye; not only in its sinful condition, but also in the sinless state. From this we infer that Adam before he fell was not without His inworking; hence that in the heavenly Jerusalem our human nature will possess Him in richer, fuller, more glorious measure. For our sanctified nature is a habitation of God through the Spirit — Eph. 2:22.'

Extending that thought and applying it, first to the glorified believer and then to the exalted Mediator he goes on: 'If, therefore, our blessedness in heaven consists in the enjoyment of the pleasures of God, and it is the Holy Spirit who comes into contact with our inner being, it follows that in heaven He can not leave us. And upon this ground we confess, that not only the elect, but the glorified Christ also, who continues to be a true man in heaven, must therefore forever continue to be filled with the Holy Spirit. This our churches have always confessed in the Liturgy: "The same Spirit which dwelleth in Christ as the Head and in us as His members"' (*The Work of the Holy Spirit*, p.110).

It may not be possible to understand what this means in any detail. Nevertheless, some general aspects of the truth may be appreciated. All the graces, powers, attributes, and gifts of human nature are exercised and used in the power of the Holy Spirit. This must be true even for the exalted humanity of the Lord Jesus. If not, then it has ceased to be true, genuine humanity and Scripture is quite clear that, in resurrection and ascension, the Lord Jesus never ceased to be man.

We have seen that the resurrection body of Jesus had changed radically. He could pass through walls, appear suddenly, be unrecognized by familiar friends. It appears that there was further change in his body at ascension. Then his spiritual, or resurrection body, became the vehicle of his mediatorial glory and splendour. This is the humanity upon which the glorified saints are to be patterned. 'But our citizenship is in heaven', writes Paul. 'And we eagerly await a Saviour from there, the Lord Jesus Christ, who, by the power that enables him to bring everything under his control, will transform our lowly bodies so that they will be like his glorious body' (Philippians 3:20,21).

The inference to be drawn from this teaching is that the body shared in the glorification of the man Christ Jesus, and that the Holy Spirit is the author and perfector of that glory. This is the thought of John Owen who says, 'It was the Holy Spirit that glorified the human nature [of Christ], and made it every way meet for its eternal residence at the right hand of God, and a pattern for the glorification of the bodies of them that believe on him.' And then, relating this work to the work of the Spirit in the incarnation Owen says, in a memorable way, 'He who first made his nature *holy*, now made it *glorious*' (*Works*, vol. 3, p.183).

In treating of the inward and outward changes which the work of the Spirit effects in believers in the process of sanctification, Paul speaks of its progress towards glory. His thought is profound, and impossible for us to probe to its depth. But it is expressed in powerful, demonstrative words that ring with conviction and certitude. 'But we all, with unveiled face, beholding as in a mirror the glory of the Lord, are being transformed into the same image from glory to glory, just as by the Spirit of the Lord' (2 Corinthians 3:18 author's translation). The corollary of this truth confirms also the Spirit's work in the glorification of Jesus. That is, if it is the work of the Spirit to change us, body and soul, into the glorious image of Christ, then we are warranted in believing that it was the same Spirit who was operative in the glorification of that humanity which provides our pattern and goal. That seems to be the conclusion that Scripture would have us draw from the information it imparts.

Entry of Christ — the perfect man

Not only did the ascension of Christ mean departure from earth in his bodily nature, it meant arrival in heaven as well. He was not the first man to arrive there, but there never before had come a man like him.

Abel was the first human being to come to heaven. According to scriptural reference to angelic interest in man's salvation, it must have been a marvellous moment for them when the first member of the human race — a fallen, sinful

145

race — appeared in the home of ultimate perfection, where all things are judged by the exquisite standard of holiness. Abel came there by faith, ransomed by grace, at the price of blood.

Peter says that 'angels long to look into these things' (1 Peter 1:12), and there must have been an inquiring into Abel's arrival that perhaps did not satisfy even their unfallen minds. It is probable that they, as well as Abel and all who followed him, were not altogether clear as to 'why' and 'how' until the events of incarnation and crucifixion began to exegete and unfold the amazing love of God to lost men, and to demonstrate the basis upon which sinners were saved and God's holiness left untainted. Old Testament believers came, as God's people still come, upon the basis of trust in a Saviour whom God has given. In their case, it was faith in one who was yet to come and a sacrifice which was yet to be offered.

In ascension something far more marvellous than even the arrival of Abel and others was happening. The Man of Galilee, the first of the new race, the last Adam came into the divine presence as none had ever come before. He came in his own right. He brought a perfect obedience with him; a perfect love to the Father's will and the Father's honour. He came having sanctified even that into which he was coming as living man, by the sprinkling of his own blood. In his coming he asked for no mercy; he had already presented the proofs of sacrifice around and upon the mercy seat. No mediator opened the door for him; the rent veil of his own body had paved the new and living way' into the presence of the Father.

Exaltation of Christ — the Saviour King

It is clear from the language that the Bible uses of the exalted Christ that he bears still the stamp of his suffering and sacrifice. These insignia are no longer unsightly or disfiguring, but 'in beauty glorified' they proclaim his death and its triumphant achievement. The fact that even in the 'centre of the throne' he is still known as the 'Lamb slain' is interpretative of his right of entrance into heaven, and session upon its throne.

In his ascension entrance to heaven, he could root his claims and rights not in the mercy but in the justice of God. He had exalted that justice in his sacrifice and had presented the sacrifice before the throne. Resurrection had ratified its acceptance. In his ascension he was taking the place already claimed by the entrance of his soul, an entrance that demonstrated the extent and fulness of his suffering to death, his bearing of the curse. It is of *that* appearance of the soul that Hugh Martin movingly writes, 'He placed his sacrifice amidst the searching blaze of heaven's divinest glory. And it endured the scrutiny. It outshone — and became the sweetest light of heaven. For "the glory of God doth enlighten it, and THE LAMB is the light thereof"' (*The Abiding Presence*, p.144).

It was on this basis that he could now freely enter the heavenly places, death and sacrifice behind him, with his complete humanity, body and soul, no longer in the state of death but united never to be separated again. He enters with an amazing history. Unfolding the chapters of his glorious biography in a word or two, he says, 'I am he who lives, and became dead, and behold, I am alive for evermore. Amen. And I have the keys of death and of hades' (Revelation 1:18, author's translation). It was into that light of which he, as Lamb of God, is source and centre, that he was exalted in mediatorial glory.

For Jesus the entrance into heaven was the entrance to its throne. It had been predicted. The messianic promises of Old Testament Scripture had done more than foretell his suffering and death; they had also spoken of his exaltation and glory. The church in the Old Testament had sung of this theme as it found expression in its Spirit-inspired song book:

> *Ye gates, lift up your heads; ye doors,*
> *doors that do last for aye,*
> *Be lifted up, that so the King*
> *of glory enter may.*
> *But who is he that is the King*
> *of glory? who is this?*

147

The Lord of hosts, and none but he,
The King of glory is.

(Psalm 24:7-8
Scottish Psalter)

That song of triumph is also the song of battle. King as he
is, he bears the marks of conflict. Why did the King — God's
one, perfect man, come to die? In the life of the perfect there
is no reason for death. The Bible tells us that death is the
wages of sin, and apart from sin there is no place for death.
Since early in the church's proclamation of this truth men
have sometimes declared that death is a necessity, part of the
natural process, nothing to do with sin. Men may declare this,
but they are unable to demonstrate it. The mystery of life,
and what constitutes self-consciousness, has eluded scientific
analysis, and therefore so also has the mystery of death.

The ultimate reason for death, as distinct from immediate,
diagnostic causes, has never been declared. Medical science
tells us that the human body renews itself once every seven
years. Why does this process not go on indefinitely? Why
does the aging process accelerate and man stoop down into
death? Science does not tell us; but Scripture does. Death
comes as the penalty for sin. The New Testament apostle
declares that this is the meaning of Genesis. 'Sin entered the
world through one man, and death through sin, and in this
way death came to all men, because all sinned' (Romans
5:12). But God did not let matters rest there. It was in the face
of sin and death that he set up his messianic King, and taught
his church in every age to sing the great, declarative anthem
of that action:

Yet, notwithstanding, I have him
to be my King appointed;
And over Sion, my holy hill,
I have him King anointed.

The sure decree I will declare;
the Lord hath said to me,

148

Thou art mine only Son; this day
I have begotten thee.

(Psalm 2:6-7
Scottish Psalter)

We have followed the King, anointed of God for the work, through birth, life, death, resurrection, and into exaltation. There is really only one answer to the question why — it was not for himself, but for others. The one who, alone of all men, did not deserve to die, has died in the place of those who ought to die. He has told us that he ascended up into the Father's home so as to prepare a place for people like us. All who trust him will be with him there (John 14:1-4). Great as that is, it is by no means all. His glory there is the pledge, as well as the pattern, for the work of the Spirit in us. There are especially two qualities of his glorified humanity which we shall share.

His glorified humanity is incorruptible and immortal. Those two features are inherent in the life of every believer from the moment of the new birth. Jesus called it 'eternal life'. Those terms tend to stir in our minds the thought of 'lastingness', of endlessness. But when Jesus used the words 'eternal life' he meant, not so much unending life as incorruptible, full, joyous life. In the sense of everlasting, all men are immortal. The Bible teaches that death does not end existence or experience for any man, not even for the lost. Eternal death is not cessation of being. It is the opposite of eternal life. It is unlikeness to the glorified humanity of Jesus. It is the loneliness of not ever knowing any peace of fellowship with God.

It is those twin thoughts of incorruptibility and perfection that Paul has in mind when expounding and explaining what he means by the redeemed bearing 'the likeness of the man from heaven' (1 Corinthians 15:47-49). He brings everything into this twofold classification: 'For the perishable must clothe itself with the imperishable, and the mortal with immortality' (v.53). When the redeemed are in that state, they have attained the 'likeness of the man from heaven'. They are

149

the very attributes of the triune God of heaven himself; he is the 'immortal God' (Romans 1:23), 'who alone is immortal' (1 Timothy 6:16).

Those redeemed have not been deified, but they have been perfectly conformed to the image and likeness of God as that is stamped upon, and mirrored in, the perfect, exalted humanity of Jesus. They take on, not only the likeness of the King, however, but the likeness of the kingdom also. Their nature is now perfectly fitted for their environment. They inhabit the world of which it is written, 'There will be no more death or mourning or crying or pain, for the old order of things has passed away' (Revelation 21:4). As if that were not enough, this also is written of that place: 'Nothing impure will ever enter it, nor will anyone who does what is shameful or deceitful, but only those whose names are written in the Lamb's book of life' (Revelation 21:27).

Session of Christ — the High Priest

The last stage of his glorification is the session on the right hand of the Majesty on high. This shows the completed, finished, accepted nature of his work for our salvation. 'After he had provided purification for sins, he sat down at the right hand of the Majesty in heaven' (Hebrews 1:3). The right hand is a scriptural figure for delegated authority. In a local sense, it is the post of honour. Both ideas are richly suggestive. They imply that Christ is exalted *by* God's right hand as the instrument, or *to* his right hand as the place of ultimate power.

Our study of the ascension and exaltation has centred on him as God's perfect man. With his session on the throne of heaven, his sitting in the presence of divine majesty, he is no longer merely the perfect man (he never *merely* was, anyway), but he is man's perfect God. We look up to him and, with all the mind and heart and soul, we endorse the confession of Thomas, 'My Lord and my God!' (John 20:28).

In heaven he is our perfect Mediator. Not only can he perfectly represent our needs there as our 'advocate with the Father' (1 John 2:1 A.V.), but he can perfectly reveal the Father to us. Apart from him man can have no true under-

150

standing of God. But in him, and the Word of God which reveals him, man finds the full and complete revelation of God. In him, God has spoken his last word to men. It is not possible for men to know God as Father, or come to him as Father, apart from the crucified, risen, and glorified Son. 'No-one comes to the Father except through me' (John 14:6). The revelation that Jesus brings is that 'God is love'.

Without his sufferings on the cross, we could never, when utterly convinced of our sin, rebellion, and total unworthiness, believe that God could love us, and love us enough to reach us and rescue us. It takes the cross; it takes the Lamb; it takes his sacrifice to persuade us of that unthinkable, unfathomable love, and to win our trust and obedience.

The Lord who did all this is no longer the sufferer but the conqueror. He has been given the place of the favourite — to put it very simply — on the right hand of God the Father. This is what he himself asks of us — the place of the favourite. His desire is to be enthroned not only in the heavenlies, but in the hearts of the sinners who become his disciples in every era. He comes into our lives as Saviour to redeem us. He comes, also, as King, to subdue us and to lead us, to reign and to rule, to fill the empty place in our hearts, to make us children of God. The title he has been given by the Father is 'KING OF KINGS AND LORD OF LORDS' (Revelation 19:16). It is most fitting. He rules and protects his church by his Spirit, and also governs it through his appointed officers. His session is not passive but active. He reigns for us.

There is only one occasion when we read of the Lord Jesus standing in heaven — that is, when Stephen, the first martyr of the New Testament church, was being stoned to death. This is how Scripture tells it: 'But Stephen, full of the Holy Spirit, looked up to heaven and saw the glory of God, and Jesus standing at the right hand of God. "Look," he said, "I see heaven open and the Son of Man standing at the right hand of God"' (Acts 7:55,56). What this means is that the exalted Christ stood up to receive one of his servants who was being rejected on earth, into the joy and everlasting glory of heaven. The significance of this is illustrated by the analogy of Hebrews 9 considered earlier. When the high priest was in the holy of holies, sprinkling the sacrificial blood, he was not permitted to sit. Session was not allowed because there was, as yet, no final sacrifice for sin. The priest's work could not be regarded as completed. The law against his sitting down in the holy of holies was continual testimony that further, future sacrifices would be required.

Again, while the priest was in the holy of holies the congregation of Israel waited anxiously outside. The only evidence they had that he was still alive and ministering within on their behalf, came from the little bells that were on the skirts of his priestly robes; those tinkled as he moved about. Had he rested, there would have been silence inside and spiritual sorrow outside. Israel waited in anxiety on those great occasions, in case the Holy One of Israel would not find their sacrifice acceptable. The sign of God's acceptance was the reappearance of the high priest himself. Then there was a shout of acclamation and Israel took peace to its heart, knowing that the sacrifice had been accepted.

One of the last glimpses of Jesus given in Scripture looks ahead to a finished redemption, and it says this, 'No longer will there be any curse' (Revelation 22:3). Why? Because the Son took the curse upon himself. 'No longer will there be any curse. The throne of God and of the Lamb will be in the city, and his servants will serve him. They will see his face, and his name will be on their foreheads' (Revelation 22:3-5). That is eloquent of the unchallenged sovereignty and lordship of God. His rule has been restored, not by being imposed upon his servants from without, but by the love which stirs their hearts within.

Conclusion

What a Saviour this Spirit-born, Spirit-anointed, Spirit-exalted Jesus is for all who come to know him and trust him. The saintly 'Rabbi' Duncan, emphasizing how closely identified with us the exalted Christ still is, even in the very midst of heaven's throne, put it strongly, if rather quaintly; 'In the exaltation of Jesus the dust of the earth has been exalted to the throne of the universe.'

In the Book of Revelation the throne is spoken of not only as the throne of God, but as the 'throne of God and of the Lamb'. There, he is given the praise of renewed and redeemed multitudes. They have been brought to know him through the work of the Holy Spirit, poured out from the throne by the ascended Lord. It is the one who ministered to him all through his earthly mission, who fitted his humanity to manifest his divine glory, who alone can exalt him in our hearts and give us the renewed will that issues in love and obedience to Jesus. It is only when we come to know him in this way that we will ever give him the glory due to him. Then, it will be gladly given: then we will join with the Spirit who praised him and taught his people to sing:

> *His name for ever shall endure;*
> *last like the sun it shall:*
> *Men shall be bless'd in him, and bless'd*
> *all nations shall him call.*
>
> *And blessed be his glorious name*
> *to all eternity:*
> *The whole earth let his glory fill.*
> *Amen, so let it be.*

(Psalm 72:17,19
Scottish Psalter)

Other Titles by Douglas MacMillan

The Lord Our Shepherd

(Now in its sixth printing)

The author's first-hand experience as a shepherd makes this study of Psalm 23 a truly inspiring book.

'spiritually and psychologically refreshing . . . unique . . .'
(*Peace and Truth*)

'warm, devotional, doctrinal preaching at its best'
(*Grace Magazine*)

'a banquet to the hungry and thirsty soul' (*Banner of Truth*)

'a very inspiring little book' (*English Churchman*)

Wrestling with God

(to appear Summer 1990)

This book is based on four addresses given by Prof. Douglas MacMillan at the Annual Conference of the Evangelical Movement of Wales at Aberystwyth. Like the addresses that were the basis for his book *The Lord Our Shepherd* these also were greatly appreciated by all those present and will prove of great devotional and practical value to all readers.

The book deals with the spiritual experiences of Jacob and especially his dealings with God at Bethel and Peniel.

Other titles published by the Evangelical Press of Wales:

MODERN-DAY PARABLES

by Mari Jones

IN THE SHADOW OF ARAN

Stories from farm life in the Welsh mountains which present spiritual truths in a vivid and imaginative way.

This popular little book has recently been relaunched in a new, colourful and compact edition, including a number of full colour photographs of the beautiful countryside surrounding the author's farm.

'I am sure that this little book will be a blessing to all who read it — enlightening the mind, awakening the imagination and moving the heart.'

D. Martyn Lloyd-Jones

and

IN THE SHELTER OF THE FOLD

A sequel to the above,
by the same author.

'An excellent publication . . . An ideal gift for Christians and for many non-Christians also.'

Evangelical Times

CHRISTIAN HANDBOOK

by

Peter Jeffery

This new handbook provides a basic introduction to the Bible, church history and Christian doctrine. In *one* handy volume it therefore provides a range of information which would otherwise only be found either in much larger and more expensive publications, or in a large number of smaller ones. Written in a plain and straightforward style, it will prove invaluable not only for the new Christian but for all who want to broaden their knowledge of the Christian faith.

- Over 90 illustrations including maps, charts, drawings and photographs.
- A comprehensive index.
- Available in hardback and paperback.

'This is a great little handbook, the best of its kind. Let every church buy a copy for each new convert; it's just what they need.' — Brian H. Edwards in *Evangelicals Now*

'This book is packed with information that every Christian needs to know. It is an ideal handbook for young people, Christians and all who wish to broaden their knowledge of the Christian faith.' — David Barker in *Grace*

Other titles by Peter Jeffery published by the Evangelical Press of Wales

Seeking God
A clear explanation of the gospel for those who are really looking for salvation in Christ.

All Things New
A simple, down-to-earth explanation of what it means to be a Christian and to live the Christian life.

Walk Worthy
Clear guidelines about prayer, the Bible, the local church, evangelism, assurance, work, marriage, money and other issues that every Christian has to face.

Stand Firm
A young Christian's guide to the armour of God.

Our Present Sufferings
An excellent little book to put in the hands of those who are going through a period of suffering.

Firm Foundations (with Owen Milton)
An introduction to the great chapters of the Bible. This book takes the form of a two-month course of daily Bible readings together with a helpful commentary on each passage.

REVIVAL

Books by Dr Eifion Evans published by the Evangelical Press of Wales:

THE WELSH REVIVAL OF 1904

A thorough but very readable study of the 1904 Revival, with a foreword by Dr Martyn Lloyd-Jones.

REVIVAL COMES TO WALES

A moving and thrilling account of the mighty working of God the Holy Spirit in Wales at the time of the 1859 Revival.

REVIVALS: THEIR RISE, PROGRESS AND ACHIEVEMENTS

A general survey of revivals and their characteristics, concentrating especially on those of the eighteenth century.

TWO WELSH REVIVALISTS

The fascinating stories of Humphrey Jones and Dafydd Morgan, the two prominent leaders during the 1859 Revival in Wales.

Further titles from the Evangelical Press of Wales relating to the subject of revival:

REVIVAL AND ITS FRUIT
by Emyr Roberts & R. Geraint Gruffydd

Studies on the nature of revival and the phenomena associated with it.

HOWELL HARRIS AND THE DAWN OF REVIVAL
by Richard Bennett; introduction by
D. Martyn Lloyd-Jones

Formerly published under the title **The Early Life of Howell Harris,** this book is an invaluable study of the early spiritual life of Howell Harris and the beginnings of the Great Awakening of the eighteenth century in Wales.

CHRISTIAN HYMNS

Paul E. G. Cook and
Graham Harrison (editors)

Over 100,000 copies of *Christian Hymns* have been sold since it was first published in 1977. The warm reception given to it by both churches and the Christian press confirm the view of many that it is one of the finest hymn-books available today.

- Comprehensive selection of 900 hymns.
- Suitable for public worship and informal church gatherings.
- Includes 80 metrical psalms and paraphrases.
- Useful children's section.
- Beautifully printed and strongly bound.

...

Words editions	**Music editions**
Standard words	Standard music
De-luxe words	Presentation music
Large-type words	(with slip case)

CHRISTIAN HYMN-WRITERS

Elsie Houghton

The stories behind some of the great hymns are often as inspiring as the hymns themselves. This fascinating book takes us 'behind the scenes' and enables us to appreciate much more those words with which we are so familiar. In brief but telling biographies, the author covers a wide range of hymn-writers from the early centuries of the Christian church down to the twentieth century. This popular work comes complete with a valuable index, and has now been reprinted with a bright new cover.

Books by Dr Martyn Lloyd-Jones published by Evangelical Press of Wales:

OUT OF THE DEPTHS

This book deals with the problem of human failure and guilt and the divine remedy of repentance. The author looks at the subject in the light of Psalm 51, and shows us exactly what repentance means, and how Christians and non-Christians alike may experience new joy in their lives. This is an immensely encouraging book.

WHY DOES GOD ALLOW WAR?

Why does God seem not to answer the prayers of His people in the face of evil and suffering? In this reprint of wartime sermons Dr Lloyd-Jones deals honestly and sympathetically with this question and answers some of our misunderstandings both about the nature of God and the nature of the Christian life.

Books on contemporary issues published by Evangelical Press of Wales:

SOCIAL ISSUES AND THE LOCAL CHURCH

Ian Shaw (editor)

Among the subjects covered by this work are: the Christian and the state, the Christian concern for education, the role of women in the church, social welfare and the local church and mission in today's world.

CHRISTIAN FAMILY MATTERS

Ian Shaw (editor); foreword by Sir Frederick Catherwood

Here is clear biblical teaching by experienced contributors on marriage, parenthood, childhood and adolescence, the handicapped child, fostering and adoption, divorce, abortion and family planning, and the care of the elderly.

THE CHRISTIAN, THE CHURCH AND DAILY WORK

Gerallt Wyn Davies

In this little book the author looks at biblical teaching regarding work, compares it with society's attitudes, and outlines what individual Christians and the church could do to be of effective help in alleviating the great social problem of unemployment.